Dancing With the Stars

(Volume Two)

God's Endless Creations

Philip M. Hudson

Copyright 2022 by Philip M. Hudson. Published 2022.
Printed in the United States of America.
All rights reserved.

No portion of this book may be reproduced,
stored in a retrieval system, or transmitted
in any form or by any means, mechanical,
electronic, photocopy, recording, scanning,
or other, except for brief quotations in
critical reviews or articles, without
the prior written permission
of the author.

ISBN 978-1-957077-18-5
Illustrations - Google Images.
This book may be ordered from
online bookstores.

Publishing Services
by BookCrafters, Parker, Colorado.
www.bookcrafters.net

Table of Contents

Foreword...1
Introduction..7
60 Scriptures With Commentary...13
Epilogue: Searching Our Roots..253
Appendix: Scripture References (Volumes One - Four).......................................259
About The Author..273
By The Author..277
Quid Magis Possum Dicire?...285
Consummatum Est!..289

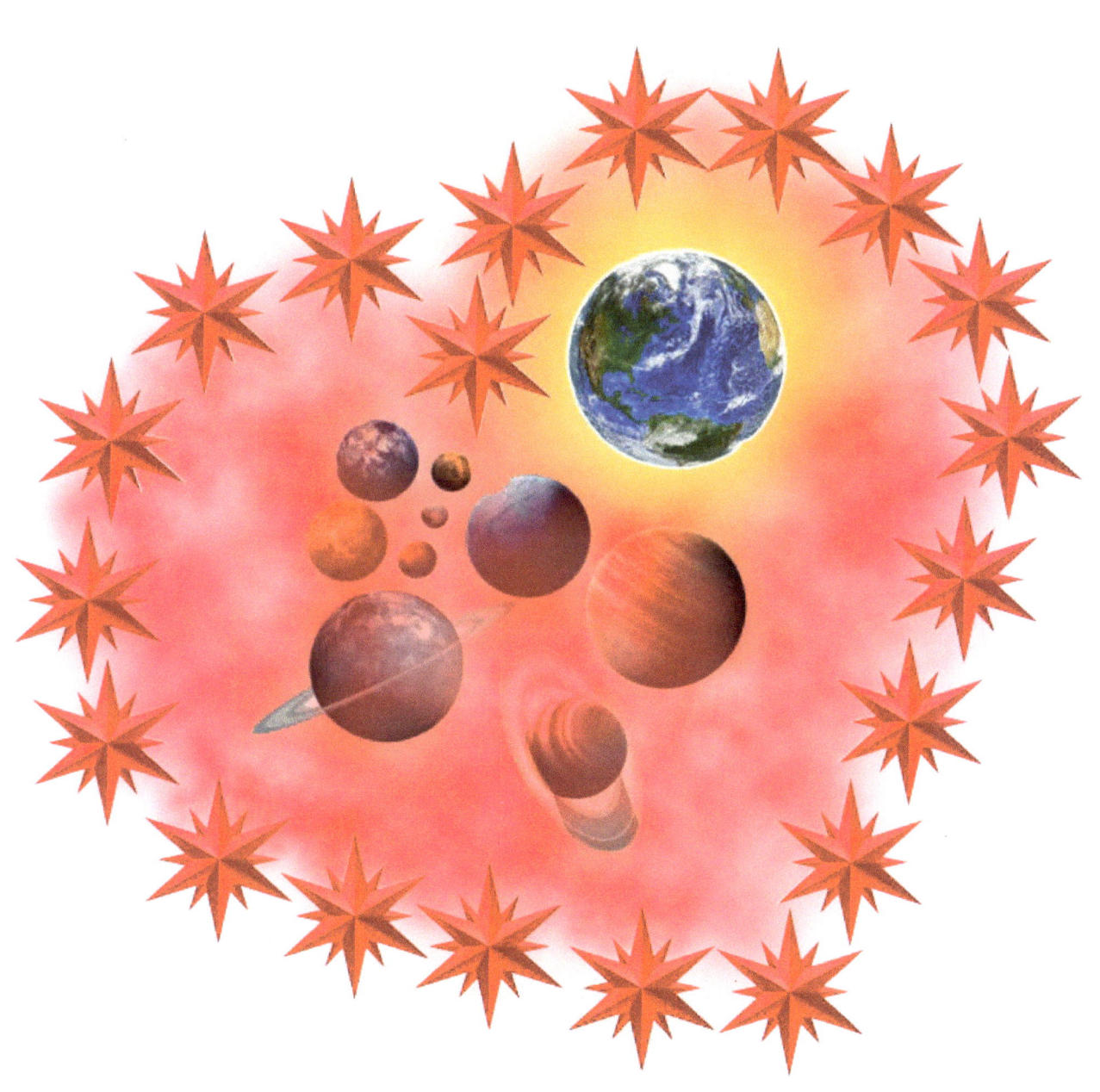

Foreword

When we pause in our reading to look up at the night sky, we ask ourselves again and again if it possible that extra-terrestrial sentient life exists somewhere out there among the stars. A tentative "yes" begs several follow-up questions: Would alien life be familiar, or unimaginably different? Might communication be possible with the inhabitants of those distant worlds? If so, might physical contact also be possible? Would it be hostile, friendly, or indifferent to our overtures? Against the background of religious dogma, what might our relationship be with extra-terrestrial beings? Might we think of them as our long-lost distant cousins? Has communication of some sort already taken place, is it now occurring, and might we reasonably expect it to be commonplace in the future?

Other questions are more esoteric, and address the possibility of communication between ourselves and the glorified inhabitants of even more elusive celestial worlds. Is there a God in heaven Who is the Fashioner and Master of the universe? If so, is communication with Him or Her possible? Might it be possible to establish face-to-face contact? Has First Contact on a level that is spiritually equivalent to subspace communication already taken place, is it now occurring, and if so, can we expect a prayerful or overt dialogue to continue? If so, what would be the conditions of such interactions, and who (or Who) would establish their boundaries?

Related questions probe the depths of our familial relationship with higher dimensional beings from the unseen world. These are metaphysical considerations that lead us to the possibility of moving from the environs of time and space to another plane of existence in eternity. Is such a transition possible? If so, would it be maturational or generational? How can we wrap our finite minds around the temporal, spatial, and dimensional variables that relate to travel to those adjacent or higher realms?

During our armchair travels to the far reaches of our minds, questions that are completely conjectural may pop up to agitate our spirits. They address the possibility of movement from one experiential level of being to higher plateaus within eternal worlds. Is it possible to move through any number of higher dimensional realities within our dynamic universe, or even within parallel universes or between multi-verses? Did our Creator haphazardly fashion our universe, worlds without end, or did He accomplish it by following a Divine Design? If He did have a Plan, might we be privy to His blueprint? Is it reasonable to assume that it is perfect in every detail? Is our galaxy only one of billions of star nurseries? Might we be so bold as to think of it as a neonatal incubator and a machine for the making of gods? Have all His children been created in His image and likeness? Is He the Grand Architect of the cosmos? Can we hope to receive divine approbation from the One Who has described Himself as both Alpha and Omega, and the Beginning and the End? As we pursue our dream of making First Contact with our relatives in the cosmos, shouldn't we also expend equivalent, or greater, energy to reconnect with our Celestial Next of Kin?

These questions are the rocks and boulders around which the entries within this volume will turbulently flow. And yet, in between the rapids there will be calm water where the Spirit will encourage us to engage in quiet reflection. We may find ourselves pinching our noses and taking a leap of faith as we plunge into the depths of our queries. If we are nimble, and if we maintain our balance as we hop from rock to boulder, we may find them to be stepping-stones that will lead us to a wonderland of independent discovery.

If you keep looking for them, you will find that the pages of this volume are peppered with elements of all these questions. Hopefully, answers will muscle their way to the forefront as you ponder and pray and wrestle for enlightenment, even as other questions germinate in your mind and spring up in the fertile soil of your serious inquiry.

On the flyleaf of his personal Bible, Sir Walter Scott penned the following lines, that apply to holy writ, but that could be interpreted as an oblique reference to profane works such as this one: "Within this awful volume lies the mystery of mysteries. Happiest are they of human race, to whom their God has given grace; to read, to fear, to hope, to pray, to lift the latch, to force the way."

I hope the entries in these four volumes will become a springboard for your own personal enlightenment, as you probe the mind of God, which is, after all, the final frontier of exploration. May you be introduced to the wonders of exciting new dimensions of experience, as you seek out new relationships and new ways of looking at life, as you catch a glimpse of eternity, and as you visualize yourself living among the stars. May you boldly go into that far country where few have gone before. For your own part, through the ministrations of the Spirit, may you better understand its realm, which is the abode of the Gods.

Introduction

God has instilled within each of us a sense of curiosity that almost compels us to stare in wonder at the night sky, as we attempt to absorb what seems to be an infinite number of stars. The Milky Way is a glowing smear of light across the heavens that is cast from 100 to 400 billion stellar furnaces. As it mesmerizes us, we ask ourselves: "Are we alone in the universe?" To think so begs credulity, and yet, we have discovered no terrestrial evidence of life elsewhere in the cosmos.

Still, myths from around the world give our galaxy its name and explain its origin. The Greeks believed it was created when suckling Heracles dribbled the breast milk of Hera, the wife of Zeus, across the night sky. It was also described as the trail to Mount Olympus, the home of the Gods, and as the path of ruin made by the chariot of the Sun God Helios. In Sanskrit, the Milky Way was called Akash Ganga (Ganges of the Heavens) and was considered sacred. Hindu cosmology explains the galaxy as an ocean of milk churned by the gods for a thousand years, to finally release Amrita, the nectar of immortal life. Heavenly Father put our knowledge of the Milky Way and the universe, estimated to contain around 600 billion similar galaxies, in a divine perspective, when He told Moses: "The heavens, they are many, and they cannot be numbered unto man; but they are numbered unto me, for they are mine." (Moses 1:37).

Although a luminous glow of light pollution hides the Milky Way from nearly 80% of those in North America, and from nearly 1/3 of the population of the world, it continues to hold us in its grasp with an almost mystical power. It dazzles our minds and figuratively illuminates every corner of our spirits.

Particle physics tells us that, at the moment of the Big Bang and the creation of the universe, there was a release of an incomprehensible number of photons, which are the basic units of electromagnetic energy. The number is 1 followed by 89 zeroes, and yet, it is essentially insignificant when compared to the intrinsic luminosity of God.

At the end of the day, when we have laid aside our scientific instruments that have been designed to probe the heavens for signs of extra-terrestrial life, we will reach the conclusion that "there is no power but of God." (Romans 13:1). It is He Who created the definable, measurable, and quantifiable photonic energy, to provide reliably consistent light in a world that would otherwise have been dark and dreary. Perhaps, this volume has captured a few rays of that heavenly aether.

Peter Pan told Wendy that she could find Neverland by taking the second star to the right and continuing straight on 'til morning. As humankind undertakes the exploration of the cosmos, we might want to heed those directions.

"The gates of hell shall not prevail against you." (D&C 21:6).

Our
genetic
code has
been scattered
across the cosmos,
publishing for all to
see the proclamation
that we are the children
of our Heavenly
Father.

Life's greatest
questions are these:
Where did we come from?
Why are we here? And where
are we going? These plumb the
very depths of the unknown
possibilities of existence.

As we open our minds to unknown
possibilities, to options we have never
considered, we envision a special place
called Kolob, "signifying the first
creation, nearest to the celestial,
or the residence of God."
(Facsimile #2).

Our brains contain
several billion petabytes of
information. Perhaps we just
need to organize the data more
efficiently, so we can better
utilize their resources to
reach our potential.

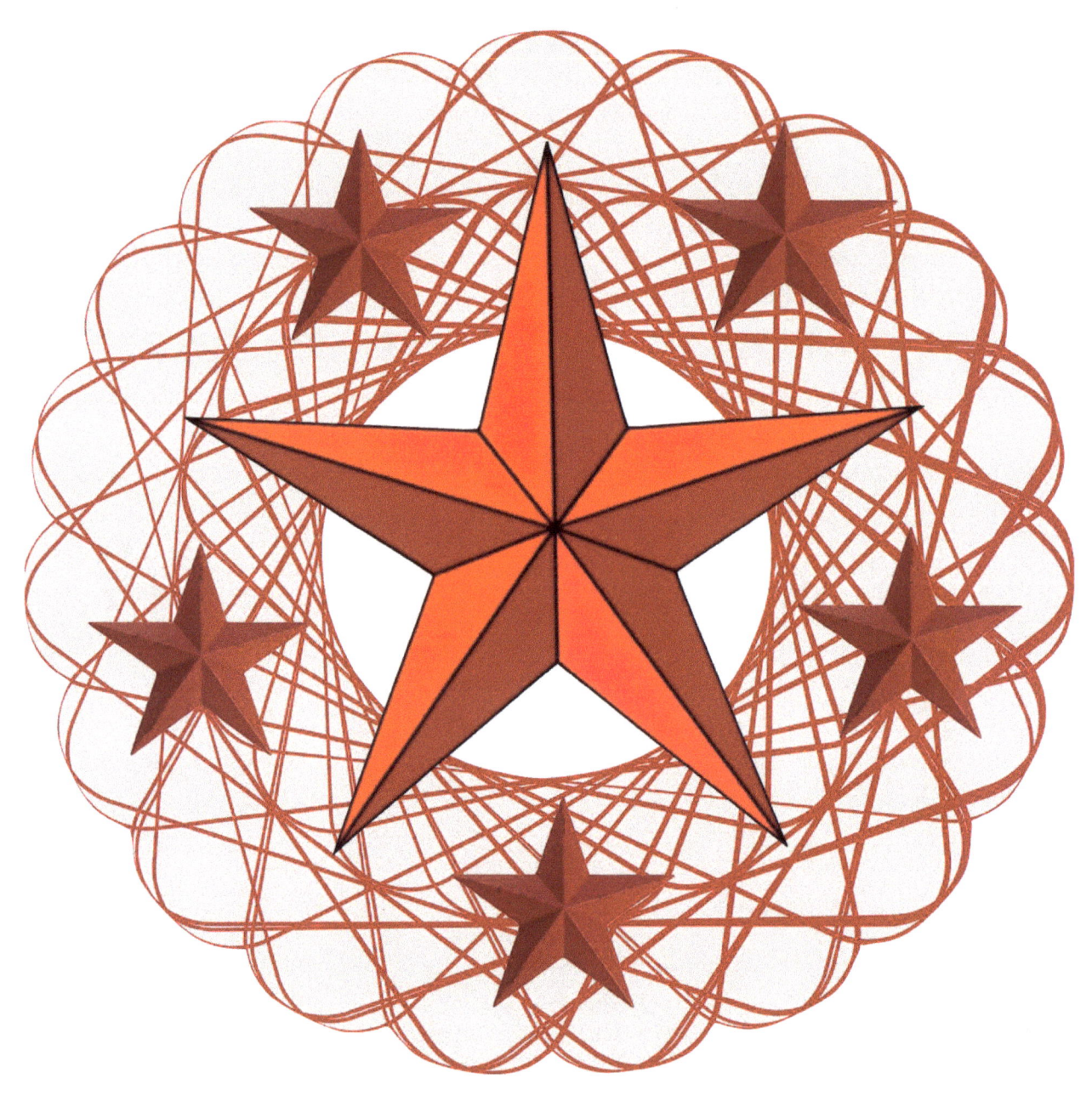

"The Lord God will disperse the powers of darkness from before you, and cause the heavens to shake." (D&C 21:6).

Heaven and
hell make for
a balanced
universe.

If life is
a dream, then
dying is the
moment you
wake up.

If you find
it hard to commit
yourself to heaven, it
could be because you
might have friends
both there and
in hell.

The perfect
orchestration
of the symphony of
life is one of our Creator's
most beautiful miracles. Our
appreciation of His cosmos helps
to reacquaint us with His celestial
design, even as we put the finishing
touches on our dissertation on life.
As we are perfected, our composition
that harmonizes with the heavens
will be recognized for the grand
ouvre and magnum opus it
has become, even God's
work and glory.

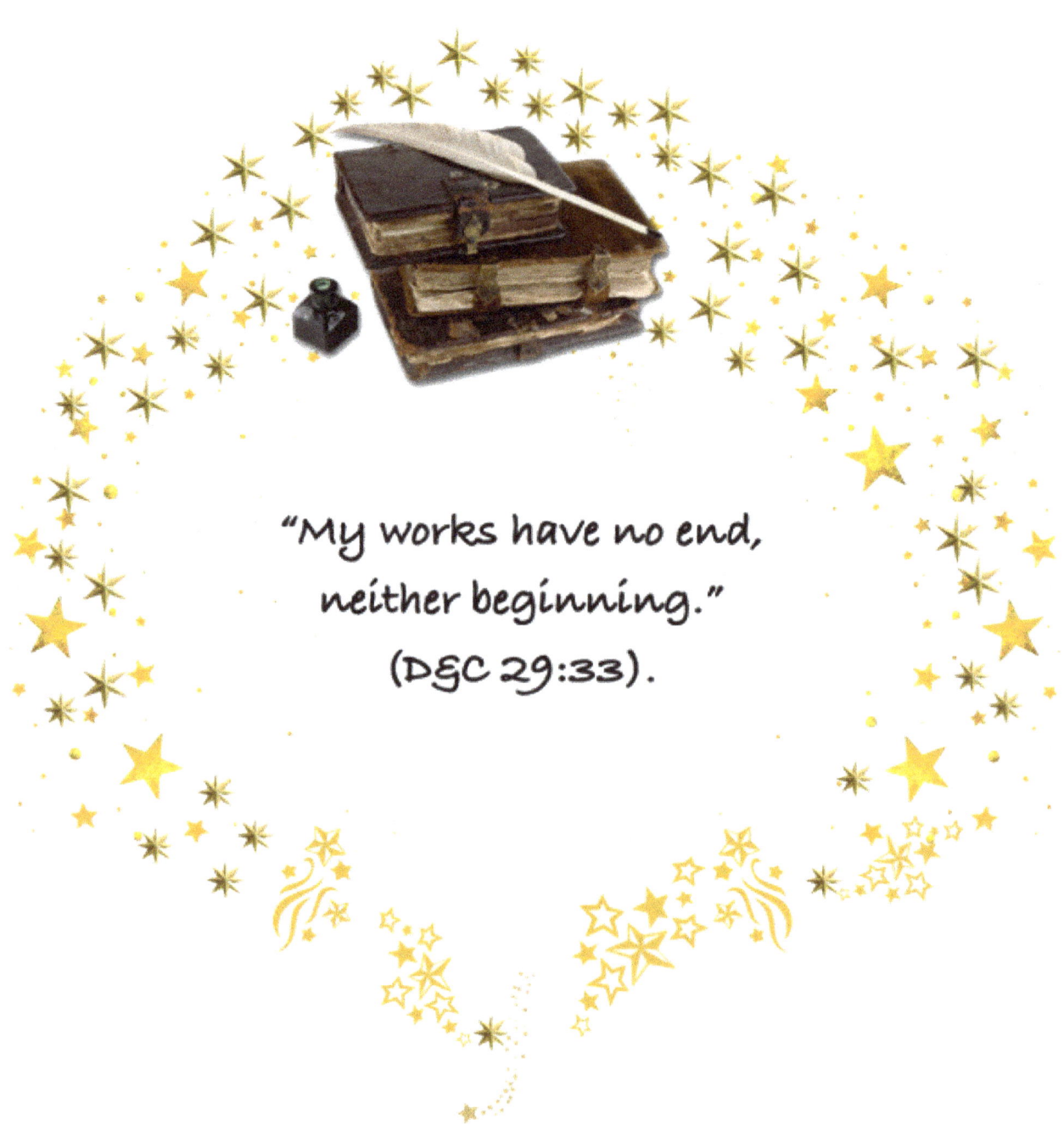

"My works have no end,
neither beginning."
(D&C 29:33).

There
is plenty of
room for moral
behavior to flex its
muscles within
the fluidity
of time.

Deep
within
each of us,
there is a divine
fire that burns the
fuel of faith to propel
us ever closer to the
heavens.

During the creation
of the universe, there was a
release of an incomprehensible
number of photons, which is as
nothing when compared to the
intrinsic luminosity of our
Father in Heaven.

"You're not
alone, you know," said Q.
"We've been watching you, and
hoping that your ape-like race would
demonstrate some growth, and give some
indication that your minds had room for
expansion ... If you're very lucky, I'll
drop by to say hello from time to
time. See you - out there."

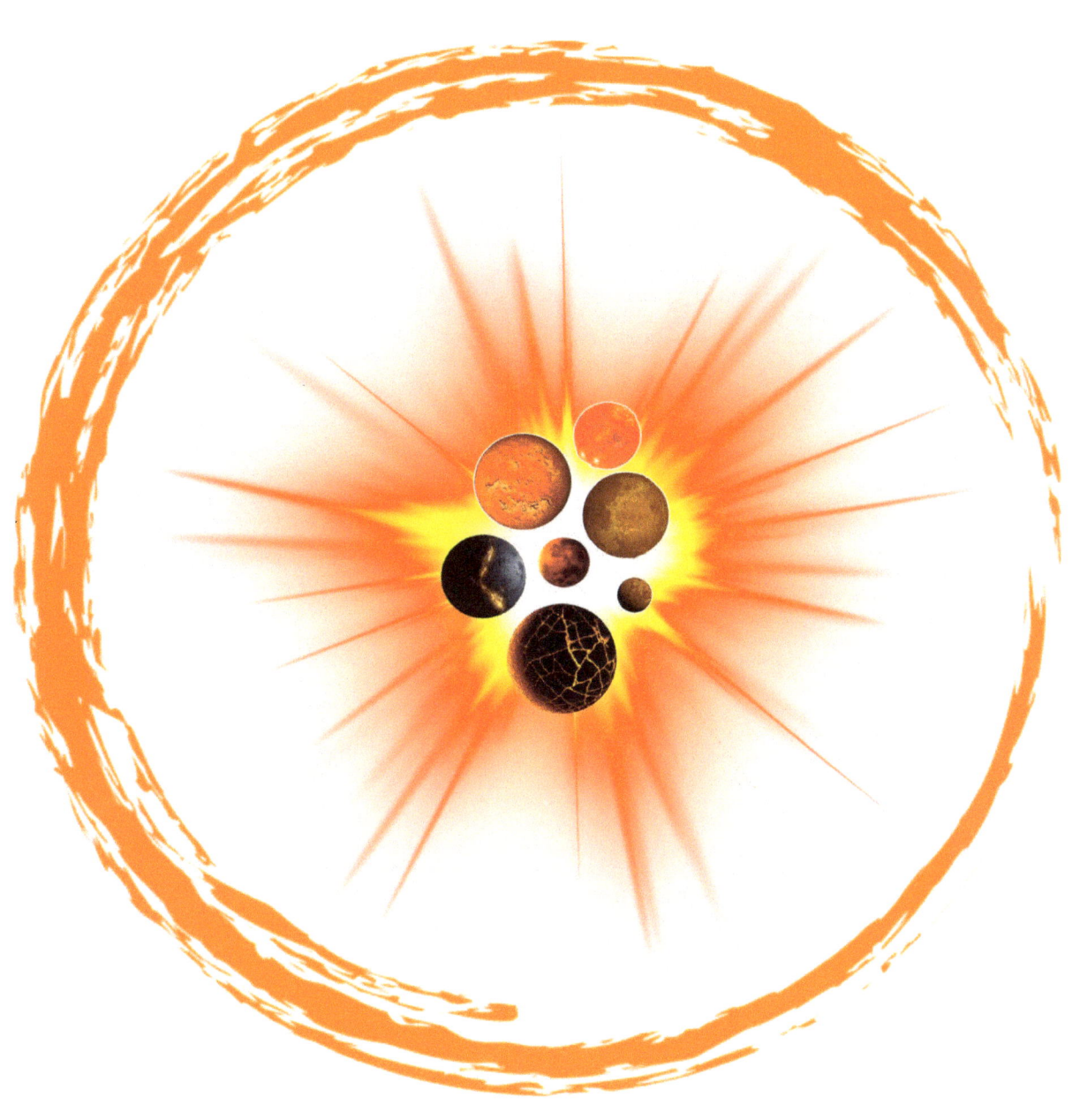

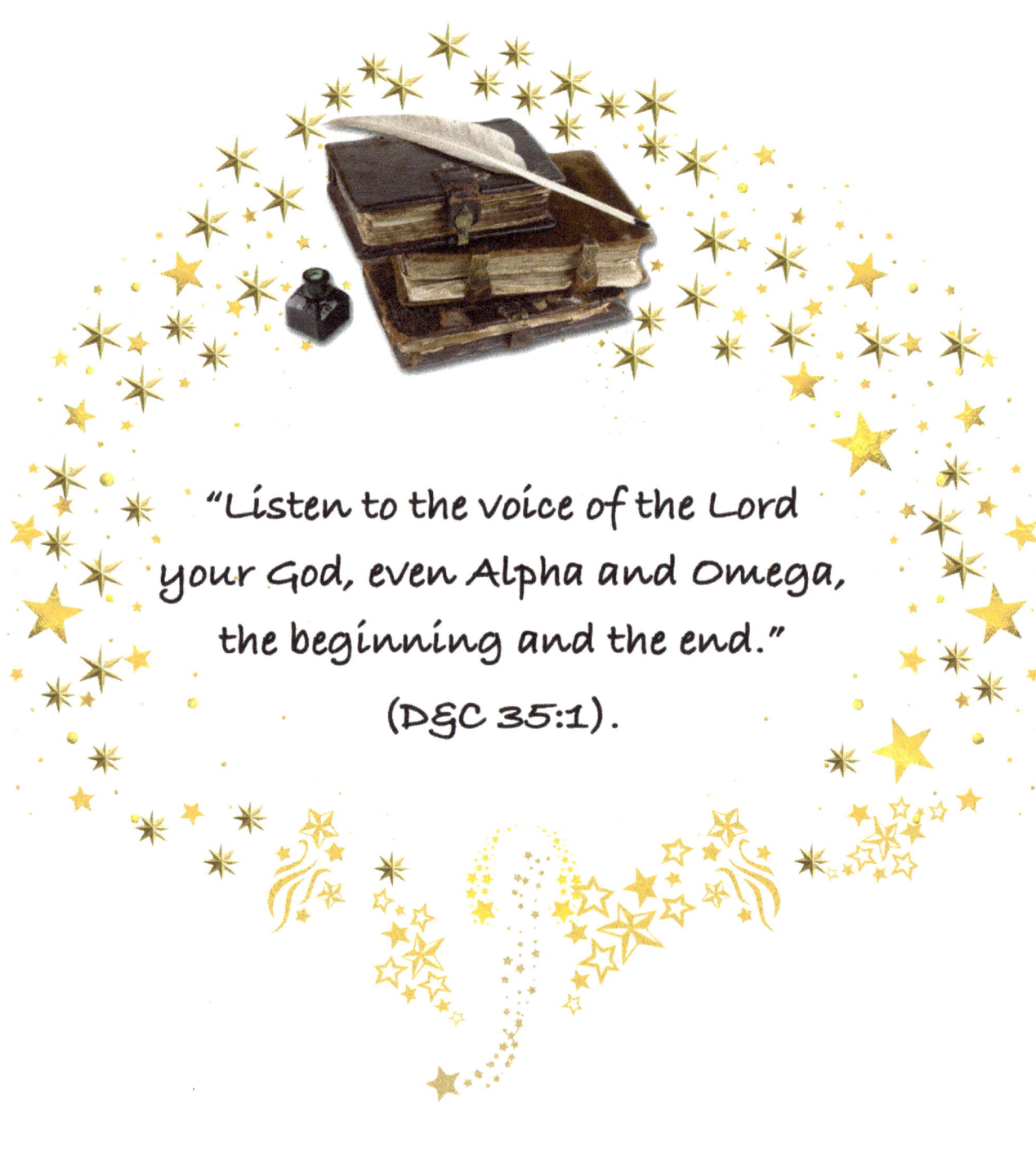

"Listen to the voice of the Lord your God, even Alpha and Omega, the beginning and the end." (D&C 35:1).

When great ideas
are presented to the world,
and they fly in the face of the
conventional wisdom of limiting
beliefs, our own thinking as well as
the intellectual prowess of entire
societies can be imprisoned.

The universe is somewhere
around 13.8 billion years old and
contains around 70 sextillion stars, many
of which undoubtedly have planets that support
sentient life. Somewhere, aliens should have evolved
into societies with the technology to either intentionally
or inadvertently broadcast their electromagnetic signatures,
their "ion trails", if you will, throughout the cosmos. Yet, back
in 1950, the physicist Enrico Fermi wondered aloud why such
evidence, that should be obvious, has not been detected. The
question he posed to the scientific community was
simply: "Where is everybody?" It has since
come to be known as "The Fermi
Paradox."

"The Great
Silence" is the
contradiction between the
astronomically high estimate of
the probability that alien life exists,
and its corresponding lack of evidence.
We ask ourselves: "Haven't we reached the point
where we should be Dancing With the Stars? By this
time, shouldn't we have already experienced the season
ending finale featuring First Contact, and shouldn't
we have a Mirror Ball Trophy to share with our
extra-terrestrial quickstep partners?"

His "course is one eternal round, the same today as yesterday, and forever." (D&C 35:2).

No
darkness
is so dense,
so menacing
or so difficult,
that it cannot be
penetrated by light.

According
to NASA, when you
look up into the night sky
every star has, on average, at
least one planet. That adds
up to a couple of hundred
billion planets in our
galaxy alone.

From the
observations made
by NASA's Kepler Space
Telescope, we can predict with
confidence that every star we see in
the sky hosts at least one planet. If we're
talking about multi-planet systems, the
number in our galaxy alone is likely on
the order of thousands of billions.

Our nearest rocky exo-planet
neighbor orbits Proxima Centauri, just over
4 light years away. If we could travel there on an Ultra
Long Range Boeing 747, the flight time from wheels up to
touch-down would be around 5 million years. One would
hope that something more substantial than a bag of
peanuts would be served during the trip.

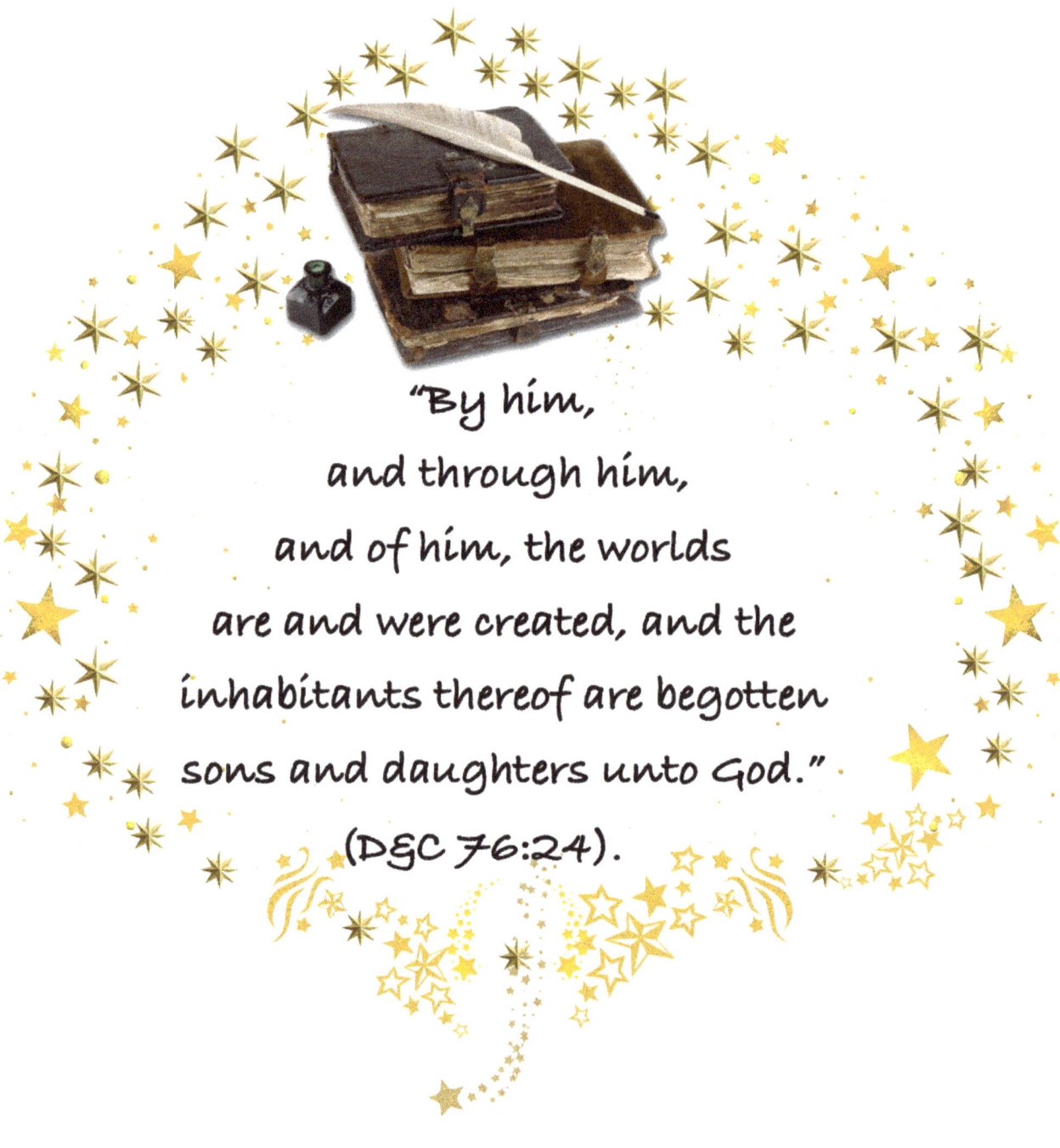

"By him, and through him, and of him, the worlds are and were created, and the inhabitants thereof are begotten sons and daughters unto God." (D&C 76:24).

We
are poised at
the edge of forever,
ready to push off onto
a vast cosmic ocean. As
we embrace the tasks that
lie ahead, we are confident
that our noble undertaking is
in harmony with our Heavenly
Father's mission statement, to
bring to pass our immortality
and our eternal life. We are
enlightened explorers, and
the Holy Spirit has given
us fire for the deed.

We have
been sent to earth
with barely enough power
to keep our pulse rates steady,
our breathing normal, and our body
temperature hovering around 37o C. But,
when it comes right down to it, batteries are
not included. We need to get our energy, drive,
motivation, zeal, insight, intuition, inspiration,
and revelation elsewhere. The sooner we come to the
realization that there is a Power upon Whom we are
utterly dependent to move us from stasis to higher
planes of awareness, the sooner He will breathe new
life into our depleted batteries. Across the cosmos,
among all of His creations, it is God Who is the
light which is in all things, that gives life
to all things, and which is the law by
which all things are energized.
(See D&C 88:13).

"The church ... stand(s) independent above all other creatures beneath the celestial world." (D&C 78:14).

In the
scriptures, we
should always be
alert to the use of the
word "suddenly," for it
often seems to presage
an other-worldly
experience.

As we gaze
toward the heavens in
amazement at the miracle
of the wash of the Milky Way,
we wonder if, somewhere out there
among the stars, there might even
now be extra-terrestrial navigators
who are making their way across
the far reaches of the galaxy with
their course set for the Celestial
Kingdom of God, perhaps
with a planned stopover
at planet Earth.

In 1990, Hubble was
launched into low-earth orbit
at an altitude of 340 miles. It will
likely remain operational until some
time between 2030 and 2040. By then,
we expect to learn much more about our
physical universe. It remains to be
seen if we will also gain a greater
understanding of our Heavenly
Father, or about the Celestial
Kingdom in which
He resides.

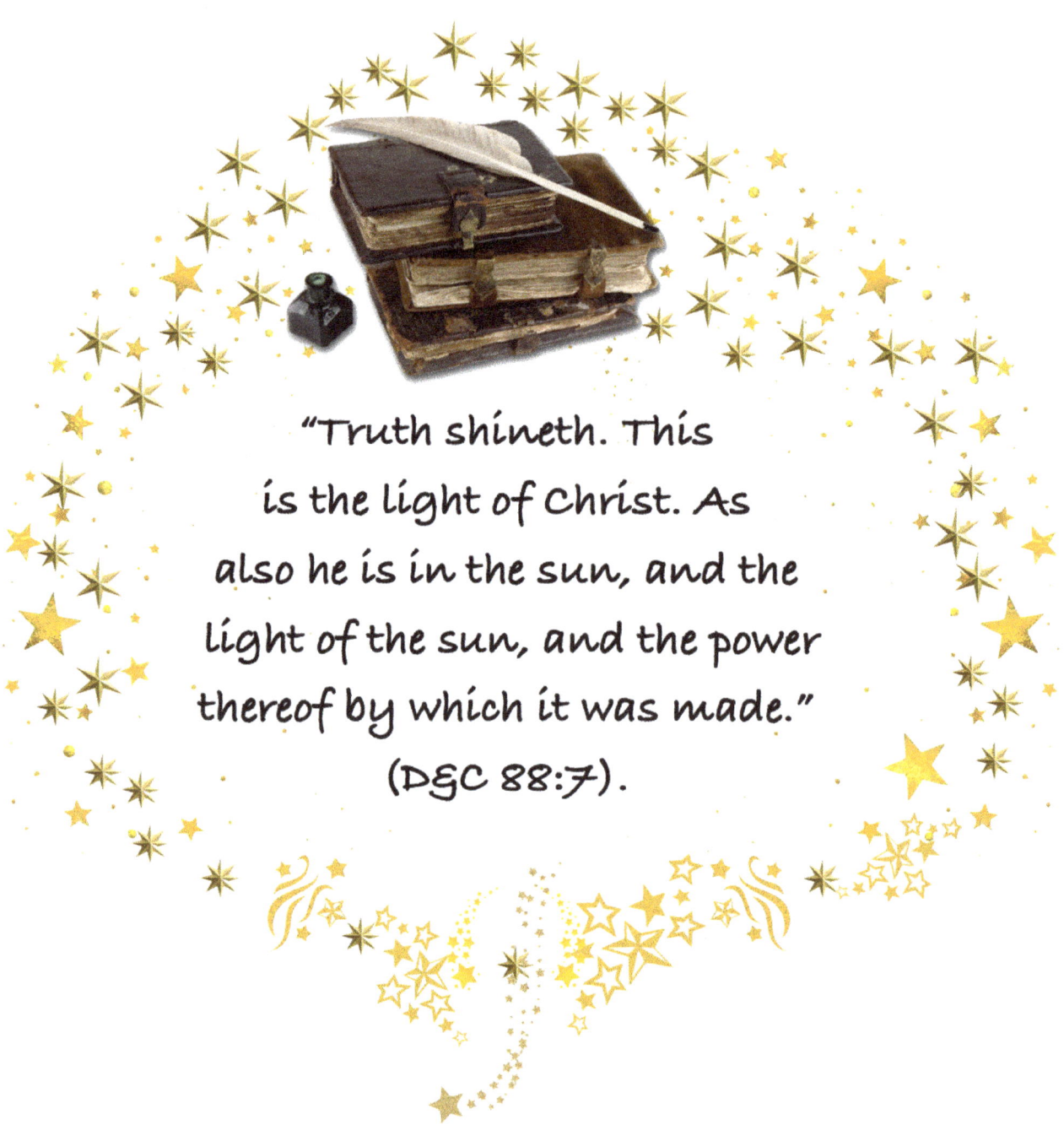

"Truth shineth. This is the light of Christ. As also he is in the sun, and the light of the sun, and the power thereof by which it was made." (D&C 88:7).

As it streaks overhead, we
can see Hubble with the naked
eye, in spite of the fact that it doesn't
have many surfaces to reflect sunlight.
It is much easier to see and feel the Spirit
from our vantage point on Earth, due to
its ability to reflect the multifaceted
light that streams down upon
us from the Celestial
Kingdom of God.

Hubble an see back in time
over 10 billion years, but it cannot
predict what will happen tomorrow. That
would require the ecclesiastical acumen of
a prophet, seer, and revelator, who teaches
known truth, perceives hidden truth,
and bears new truth.

Aesop cautioned the Athenians:
"Beware lest you lose the substance
by grasping at the shadow." The Hubble
Space Telescope was launched from the shuttle
bay of Discovery in 1990. It is the size of a large
school bus and cost $1.5 billion. After its deployment,
it was discovered that because the mirror had been ground
incorrectly, it was unable to focus on its targets. Its images
were fuzzy, and it would have become costly space-junk had a
subsequent shuttle mission been unable to correct the problem.
Even now, when we marvel at breathtaking photos of distant
galaxies taken by Hubble, we recall the blurry images it
produced before its repair. If we hope to wander among
the stars one day, we must maintain our focus.

"The curtain of heaven (shall) be unfolded, as a scroll is unfolded after it is rolled up, and the face of the Lord shall be unveiled."

(D&C 88:95).

The mirror of Hubble had been very precisely ground to the wrong shape. But, in a stellar example of the principle that there must needs be opposition, it was that accurately defined shape that led to the design of new optical components that exhibited exactly the same imprecision, but in the opposite sense, to be added to the space telescope at a subsequent servicing mission. It would be like adding a set of glasses to correct Hubble's nearsightedness.

Sometimes, the "mirror" in our finely tuned and precisely engineered optics has become so contaminated or compromised by sin, and lies so far outside our mission parameters, that it no longer conveys accurately focused images of the world to our sensory array. We conduct our daily activities based on misinformation or severely compromised data streams. Thus, our performance is neutralized. We operate at levels well below our potential. As was the case with the Hubble Space Telescope, we need the spiritual equivalent of NASA's ingenious "Corrective Optics Space Telescope Axial Replacement" to eliminate our spiritually spherical aberration. We need someone to step up with a solution to our problem. We need the active intervention of a Savior, Who will apply the power of Atonement to address our inadequacy. His sacrifice was a COSTAR, in the sense that He became "a bright and morning star" (Revelation 22:16) to whom we might look for our redemption and our renewal, when we discover to our horror and embarrassment that the mirrors that serve as our windows on the world have become fuzzy, not that they have been ground incorrectly, but that their clarity has become distorted by sin.

"They also shall be caught up to meet him in the midst of the pillar of heaven."
(D&C 88:97).

Over 15,000 papers based on Hubble data have been published in peer reviewed journals, while many of them have been referenced in conference proceedings. That is impressive, but it pales in comparison to what the Lord revealed almost two hundred years ago. Speaking of His anointed, He declared: "Whatsoever they shall speak when moved upon by the Holy Ghost shall be scripture, shall be the will of the Lord, shall be the mind of the Lord, shall be the voice of the Lord, and the power of God unto salvation." (D&C 68:3-4).

The wondrous Hubble Space Telescope has helped resolve questions relating to the age and the expansion of the universe, black holes, the solar system, the mass and size of the Milky Way, and supernovas. But it doesn't address the subject of gaining wisdom by faith. (See D&C 88:118, & James 1:2). Moroni exhorted us, including Hubble astronomers, that we should seek to establish a relationship with our Father in Heaven. If we would approach him "with real intent, having faith in Christ, He (would) manifest the truth" to us. We would then be inspired to draw upon the limitless reserves of the Holy Ghost to "know the truth of of all things." (Moroni 10:4-5). Not only those of faith, but also scientists, need to understand that it is Jesus Christ Who is the "creator of all things from the beginning." (Helaman 14:12).

"Men were made by him."
(D&C 93:10).

The Hubble telescope can 'see' billions of light years into our past, almost back to the moment of creation at the Big Bang, but it cannot gaze into heaven for five minutes. If it could do that, we "would know more than (we) would by reading all that has ever been written on the subject." (Joseph Smith).

When the great antediluvian patriarch Enoch spoke the word of the Lord thru the power of the priesthood, "the earth trembled, and the mountains fled, even according to his command; and the rivers of water were turned out of their course; and the roar of the lions was heard out of the wilderness." (Moses 7:13). The commotion that Moses described was the manifestation of cosmic confusion and galactic turmoil.

Just because the laws that govern our physical universe define entropy, they do not necessarily doom us to isolation in a cosmos headed in the direction of chaos and confusion. There are bounds and conditions that might yet enable us to find it within our reach to thread the eye of the needle and walk the line past the seemingly inexorable, unrelenting, unstoppable, unavoidable, and unalterable demands of disproportion that might, in other circumstances, doom our dreams of travel among the stars to nothing but fanciful imaginations.

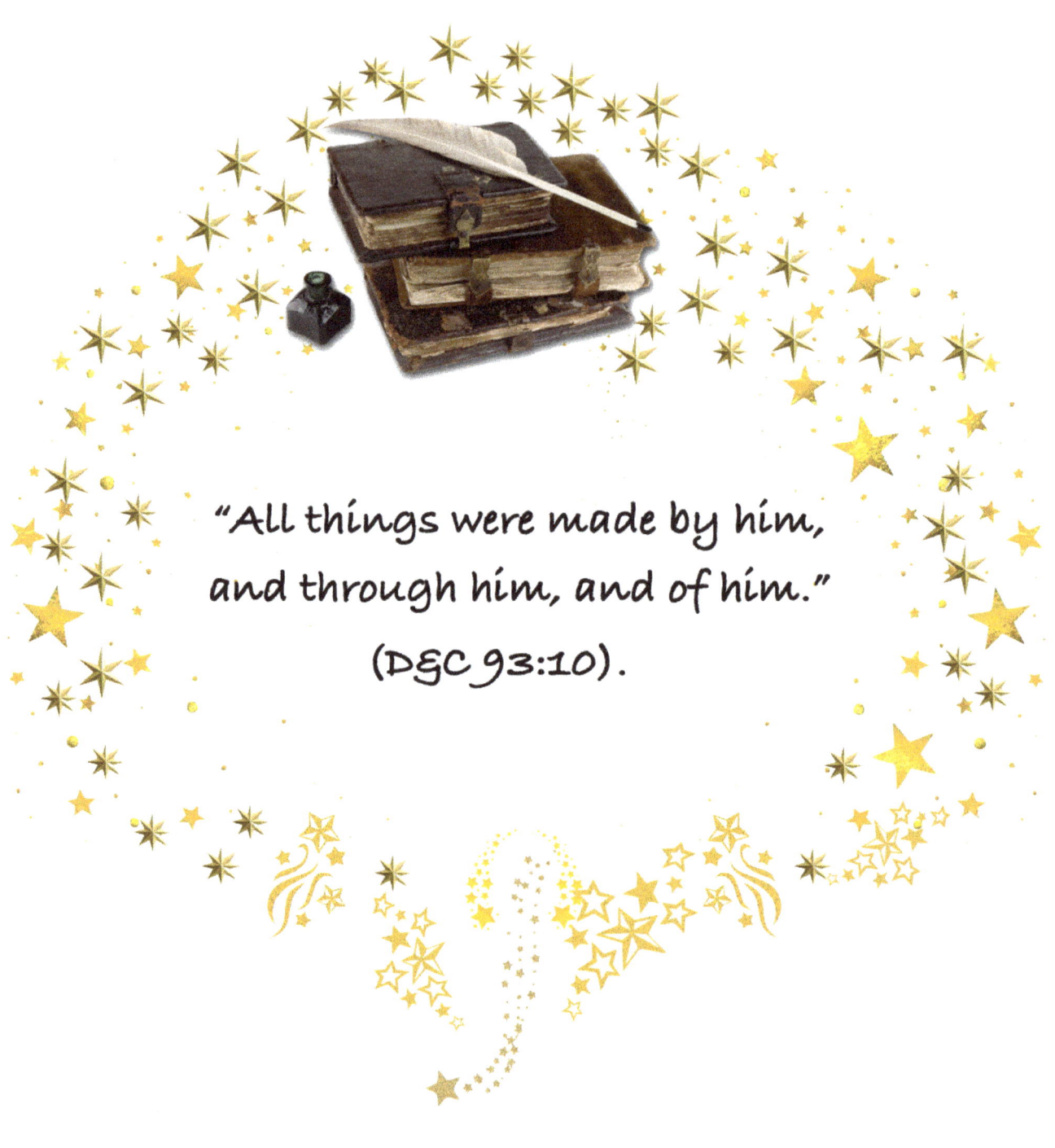

"All things were made by him,
and through him, and of him."
(D&C 93:10).

The lights in the sky are holes in the floor of heaven. If we shoot for the moon and miss, we'll still land among its stars.

If you've ever wanted to observe a black hole, look up this evening and locate the constellation Sagittarius. It lies near the center of the Milky Way. Within it, there's a raging black hole whose gravity holds all the billions of stars in our galaxy together.

We don't need to witness a burning bush on Sinai or to hear thunder emanating from its summit to realize that we are not alone in the universe. "The earth rolls upon her wings, and the sun giveth his light by day, and the moon giveth her light by night, and the stars also give their light, as they roll upon their wings in their glory, in the midst of the power of God. Unto what shall I liken these kingdoms, that ye may understand? Behold, all these are kingdoms and any man who hath seen any or the least of these hath seen God moving in his majesty and power." (D&C 88:42-47).

"In the beginning, God created the heaven and the earth. And the earth was without form, and void." (Genesis 1:1-2).

Job asked questions that most of us have posed: "Canst thou find out God? Canst thou find out the Almighty?" His answer was one for the ages. In our day, we would say that it explored a frontier that bordered on the unknown possibilities of existence. God's habitation, he wrote, "is as high as heaven (and) the measure thereof is longer than the earth, and broader than the sea." (Job 11:7 & 9).

Limiting beliefs smother our opportunities to experience our lives abundantly. When our expectations are lower, we paint ourselves into conceptual corners, and we restrain our creative talents to a few expressions within the bounds of a restrictive rational reality. Turning our backs to the light of inspiration, we think we have it all, when all that is really before us are elusive shadows, flickering illusions, and brutal caricatures of reality. When we are caught up in telestial traffic jams and doctrinal dilemmas, we are less receptive to the notion that it is possible to Dance With the Stars, but when we muster the faith to think expansively, the likelihood of making First Contact with the Spirit increases exponentially. If that happens, it no longer seems unreasonable to think that we might one day sit down with our galactic neighbors who have been touched by the better angels of their nature, just as we have been, to carry a magic light in their hearts that is powerful enough to illuminate a pathway leading past nebulae and star clusters, all the way to the source of their being.

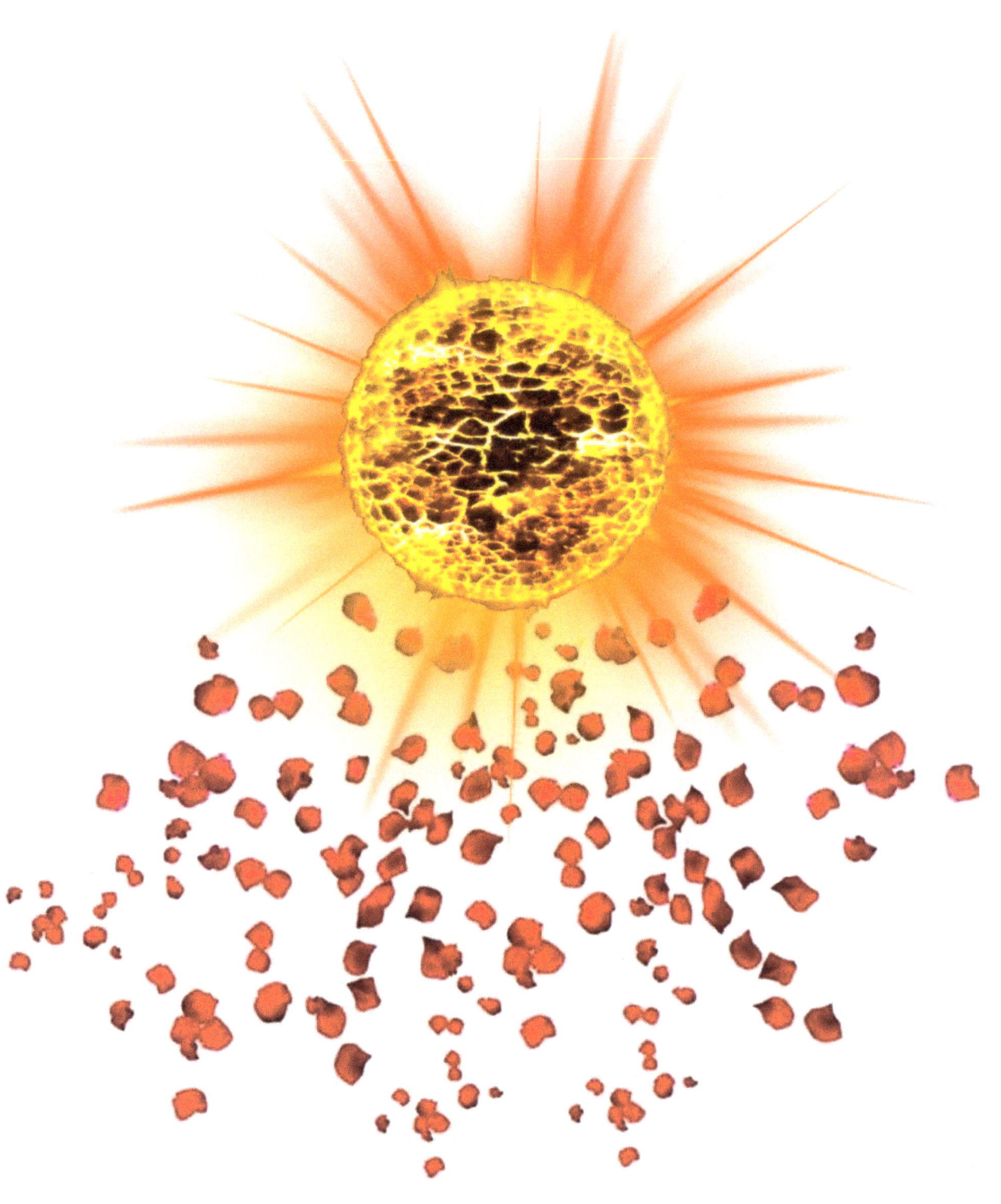

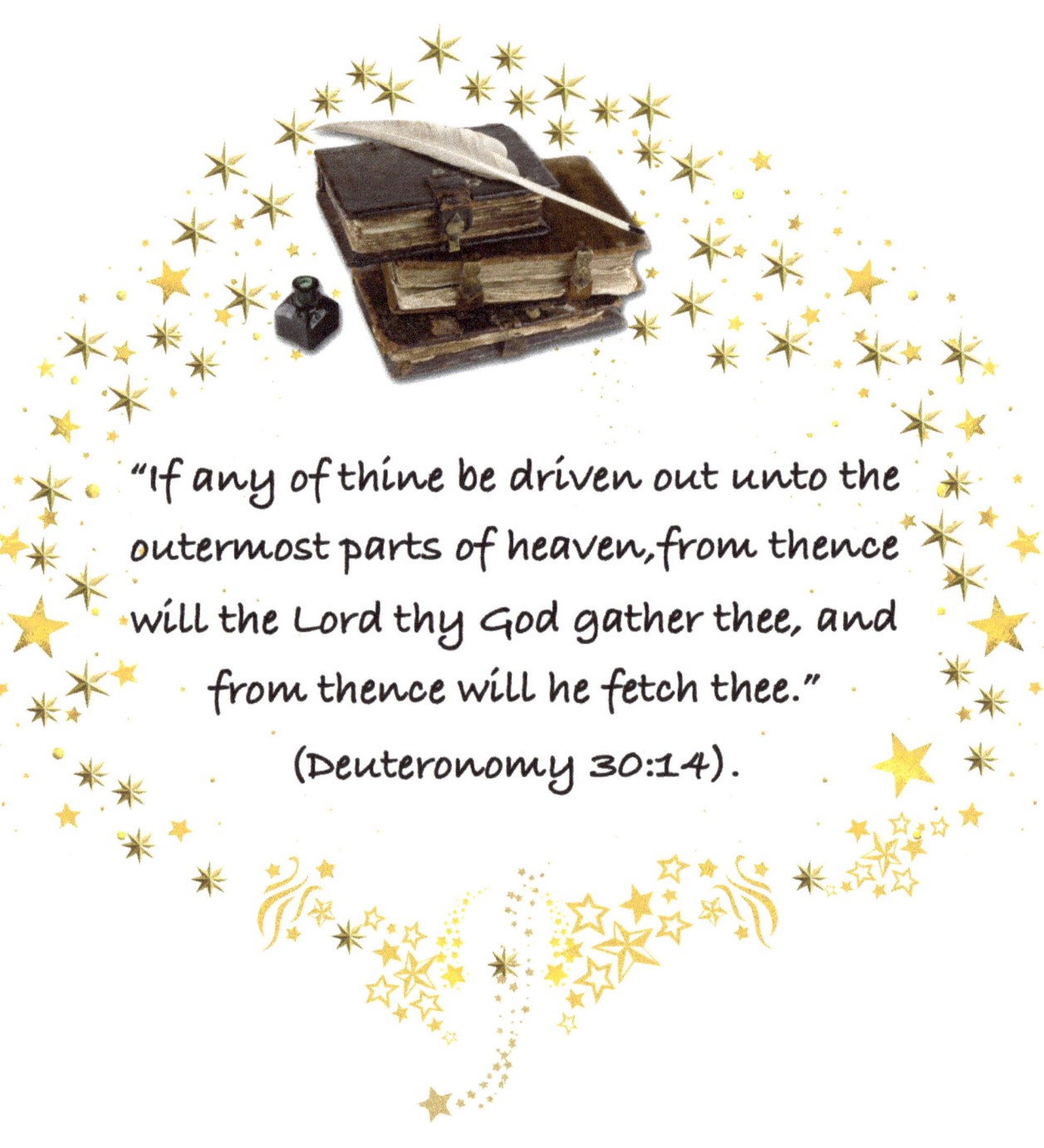

"If any of thine be driven out unto the outermost parts of heaven, from thence will the Lord thy God gather thee, and from thence will he fetch thee."

(Deuteronomy 30:14).

"The worst enemy thou canst meet, wilt thou thyself always be." (Friedrich Nietzsche). Each of us is confined to a world of our own making, and most of us are trapped within narrowly defined perceptual prisons we have created for ourselves. Its walls are reinforced with the razor-wire of limiting beliefs, those stories we tell ourselves that cause us to sabotage our own best efforts. They can damage and even cripple our lives, diminish our abilities, compromise our progress, and keep us from attaining our goals. Although all of us have limiting beliefs, we have the power to change them. Most of us don't even realize it's possible, and are not aware that we have made unconscious decisions about what to believe and what not to believe, especially when these determinations are related to the expansion of our understanding of what had heretofore been the precincts of the unknown possibilities of existence.

When our Earth, along with the cosmos, was organized, our Father in Heaven reached out from the eternal vantage point of His kingdom and re-set the celestial clock. By doing so, He set in motion The Plan of Salvation. The days of our lives, its second, minutes, and hours, were inextricably interwoven into the fabric of His divine design.

"Whereupon are the foundations (of the earth) thereof fastened? Or who laid the corner stone thereof, when the morning stars sang together, and all the sons of God shouted for joy?" (Job 38:6-7).

In a coming day,
we may find that quorum
sensing on a cosmic scale has become
common. Even now, our terrestrial efforts
to discover the existence of life elsewhere in
the galaxy might simply be the evidence of
our innate sense of quorum. If so, we may
already intuitively know the answers to
the questions that gnaw at our spirits,
beginning with: "Are there others
who are like us somewhere out
there among the stars?"

As we begin to
brush up against the stars
in the heavens, we are awakening
to a greater vision that is blinding at
first, But as our eyes adjust to the light, we
will be surprised to see the world as it really is,
perhaps for the very first time. As we begin to feel
the creative expression of the power that is within us,
we will recognize it as an intrinsic energy that brings
us closer to the heavens. We will feel that we are not alone
in the universe, but more than that, we will recognize God's
divine potential within us. We will feel the confidence to ask
seemingly simple and innocent questions whose profound
answers and implications will shake our world. Our new
perspective will spread as ripples radiating outward from
a rock thrown into the still waters of our perceptual
pond. Our questions will feel intensely personal
but they will have broad applications They
may be child- like in their simplicity,
but within the answers, if we listen
very closely, we will be able
to hear what God is
thinking.

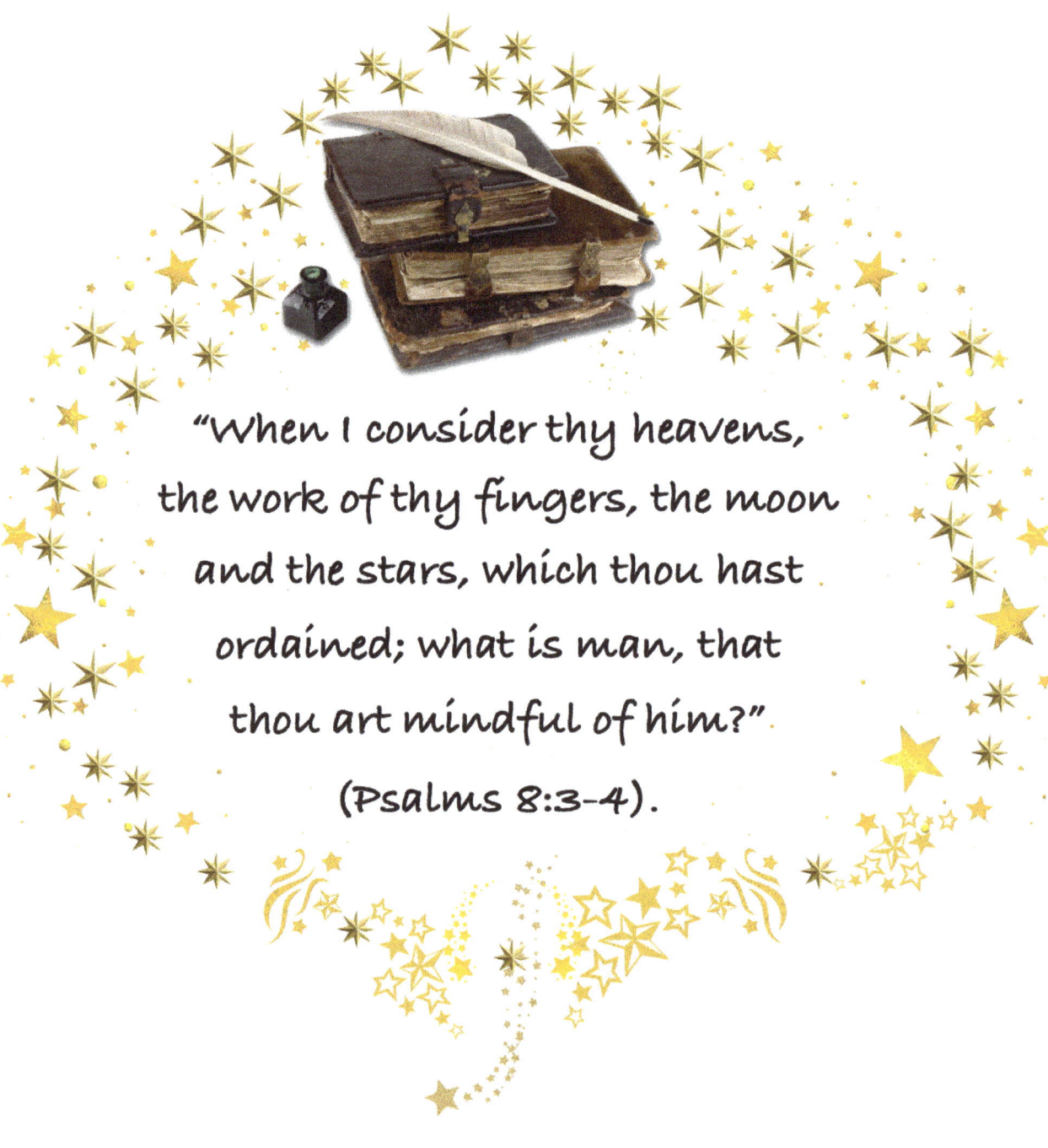

"When I consider thy heavens, the work of thy fingers, the moon and the stars, which thou hast ordained; what is man, that thou art mindful of him?" (Psalms 8:3-4).

Peter Pan
revealed to Wendy that she could
find Neverland by taking the second
star to the right and continuing
straight on 'til morning.

The inner beauty that
radiates from the faces of the
righteous is the faint afterglow of
celestial glory. But it can be enough to
act as a beacon to unerringly guide those
who are seeking the truth past the reefs and
shoals upon which they might otherwise run
aground upon God's endless creations. That
light can then guide those who have become
lost to the safe harbor of the Gospel, even if
they undertake their journey from the
farthest reaches of a vast and
turbulent galactic ocean.

Within Heavenly Father's Plan to quicken
our spirits and invigorate our lives, the Light of
Christ is an imperative. It permeates the universe, whose
architect is our Savior. His wonders include the "Pillars of
Creation," elephant trunks of interstellar gas and dust in the
Eagle Nebula. In an 1857 sermon entitled "The Condescension
of Christ," London pastor Charles Spurgeon coined the phrase
to describe the physical world and the force stemming from
the Divine that binds it all together. "Now wonder, ye
angels," Spurgeon wrote of the birth of Christ, "the
Infinite has become an infant; He, upon whose
shoulders the universe doth hang, nurses
at his mother's breast; He who created
all things and bears up the
Pillars of Creation."

Thou "maketh his angels spirits, his ministers a flaming fire: Who laid the foundations of the earth, that it should not be removed for ever." (Psalms 104:4-5).

Our
heaven-sent
promise is this: by
obedience to celestial
principles and doctrine
we find our way in "the life
and the light, in the Spirit and
the power, sent forth by the will of
the Father through Jesus Christ, his
Son." (D&C 50:27). Somewhere within
the vast reaches of the galaxy, certainly
there are others like us, who hope to inherit
dominion and glory and a kingdom. But
they might attain the spiritual stature of
their Father and our Father only if they
are cleansed from all sin, by the power
of the Atonement, in the refining
light that flows from the Savior
of worlds without end.

Those who find themselves in the
grasp of darkness because they have refused
the Gospel and turned against the Savior, may
as well be adrift in the frigid vacuum of space. Their
habitations will eventually become desolate, forlorn, and
forsaken, as nature withholds her bounties. If we alienate
ourselves from God, all the world becomes our enemy, and
the Milky Way itself may seem a dark and a foreboding
expanse. Without the Light of Christ, it can be a raging
interstellar sea, and a galactic graveyard filled with
strange dwarf stars, fearful solar flares, terrifying
supernova, deadly bursts of gamma radiation,
rogue black holes, strange magnetars, and
the terrors of cosmic cannibalism.

"Thy kingdom is an everlasting kingdom, and thy dominions endureth through all generations."

(Psalms 145:13).

"All
things bright and
beautiful, all creatures
great and small, all things
wise and wonderful, the Lord God
made them all. Each little flower that
opens, each little bird that sings, He
made their glowing colors; He
made their tiny wings."
(Cecil Alexander).

"If the universe was
created on January 1st, it was not
until May that the Milky Way was
formed. Our Sun and Earth appeared in
mid-September. Life arose soon thereafter.
Humans appeared on the cosmic calendar
in the last few seconds of the last
minute of December 31st"
(Carl Sagan).

The Bright
Star Catalogue
lists over 9,000 celestial
objects that can be seen with
the naked eye on a dark and
moonless night. There are other
scientists who feel that number
is unrealistically high. In any
event, we can see only half that
many (in each hemisphere).
All but a few are in our
own Milky Way
Galaxy.

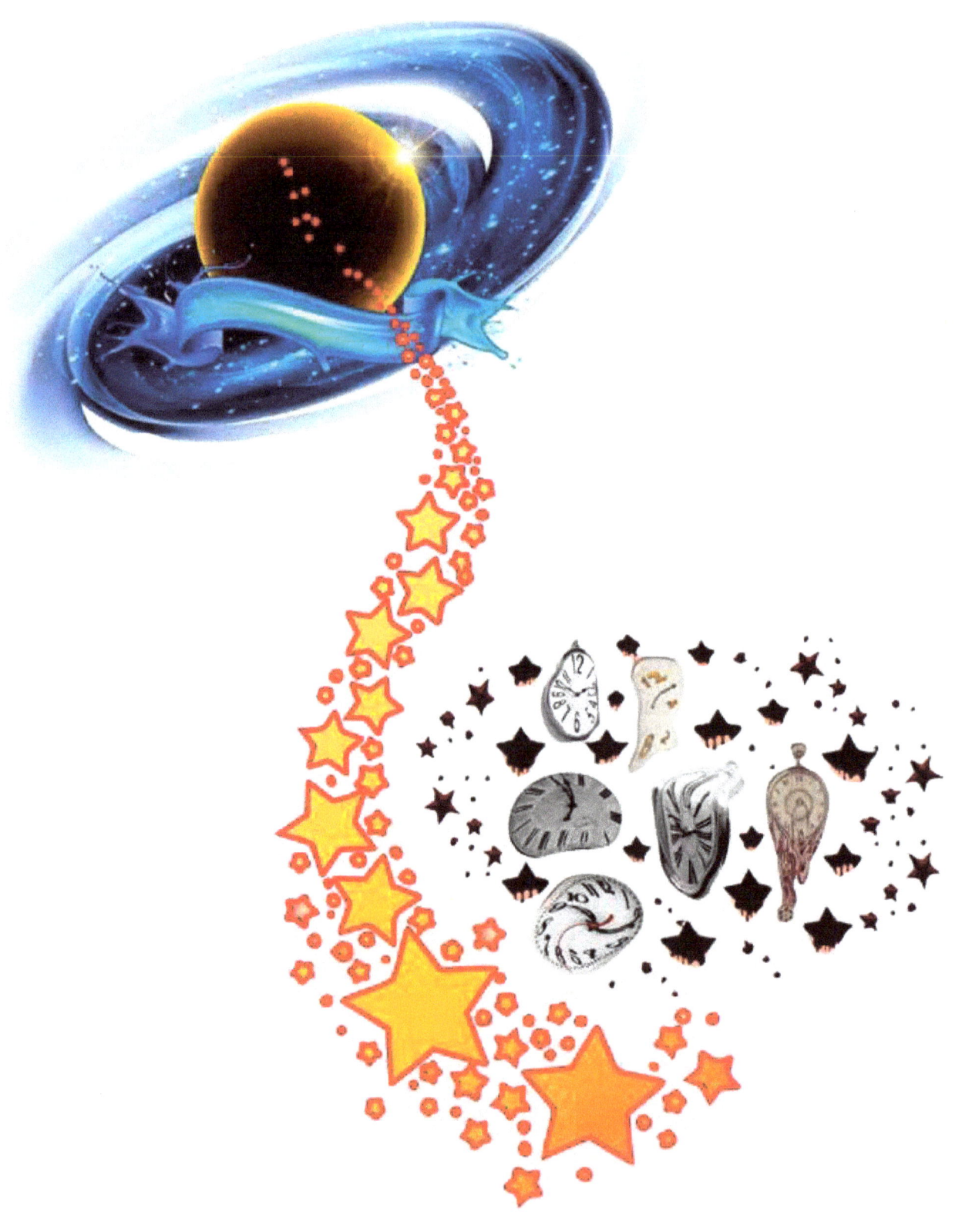

"Great is our Lord,
and of great power: his
understanding is infinite."
(Psalms 147:5).

Joseph Addison spoke of "the spacious firmament on high, with all the blue ethereal sky and spangled heavens a shining frame." Thus, is the power of God displayed, that is "published to every land the work of an almighty hand, while all the stars that round Him burn, and all the planets in their turn, confirm the tidings as they roll, and spread the truth from pole to pole", that Jesus Christ is the creator of the heavens and earth, and all that is in them. (See 2 Nephi 2:14)).

"Twinkle, twinkle, little star, how I wonder what you are! Up above the world so high, like a diamond in the sky." (Jane Taylor, 1806).

Wrote the poet: "The stars are mansions built by Nature's hand, and, haply, there the spirits of the blest dwell, clothed in radiance, their immortal vest. A huge ocean shows within its yellow strand a habitation marvelously planned for life to occupy in love and rest." (William Wordsworth). Each one that burns so brightly in the heavens has been created by our Father to be a kingdom of glory, to be the abode of the righteous.

"The eyes of the Lord are in every place."
(Proverbs 15:3).

It is a fact that,
since the spring of 1820,
the evidence of extra-terrestrial
intelligence has been staring us in
the face. Alas, it has been more than
two hundred years since Joseph Smith
laid down his testimony on the altar of
faith, and yet there are still very few in
the world who rightly understand the
nature of heavenly beings. But if we
do not understand the character of
our Heavenly Father, how can
we ever hope to understand
ourselves?

What would happen if
were able to carry our own space
with us in a warp bubble? If we could do so,
there would be no time dilation. This is because
the speed of light would be linked to the environment
within the bubble, and time would remain constant, but
only for as long as we were able to maintain a stable visual
orientation. Relative to space that was outside the environment
of our bubble, we would remain at rest, which agrees with the claim
that the speed of light is constant. This explains why it is impossible
to determine speed through space without another body to which we
can relate for reference. The only scenario in which the universe
could have a cosmic speed limit that is linked to the speed of
light, would be if there were absolute space and absolute
time, which was the Newtonian concept of a static
universe. Thanks to Einstein, that unchanging
universe no longer seems to exist, if it ever
did. As we now understand it, space is
constantly expanding, and it has
neither temporal nor spatial
boundaries.

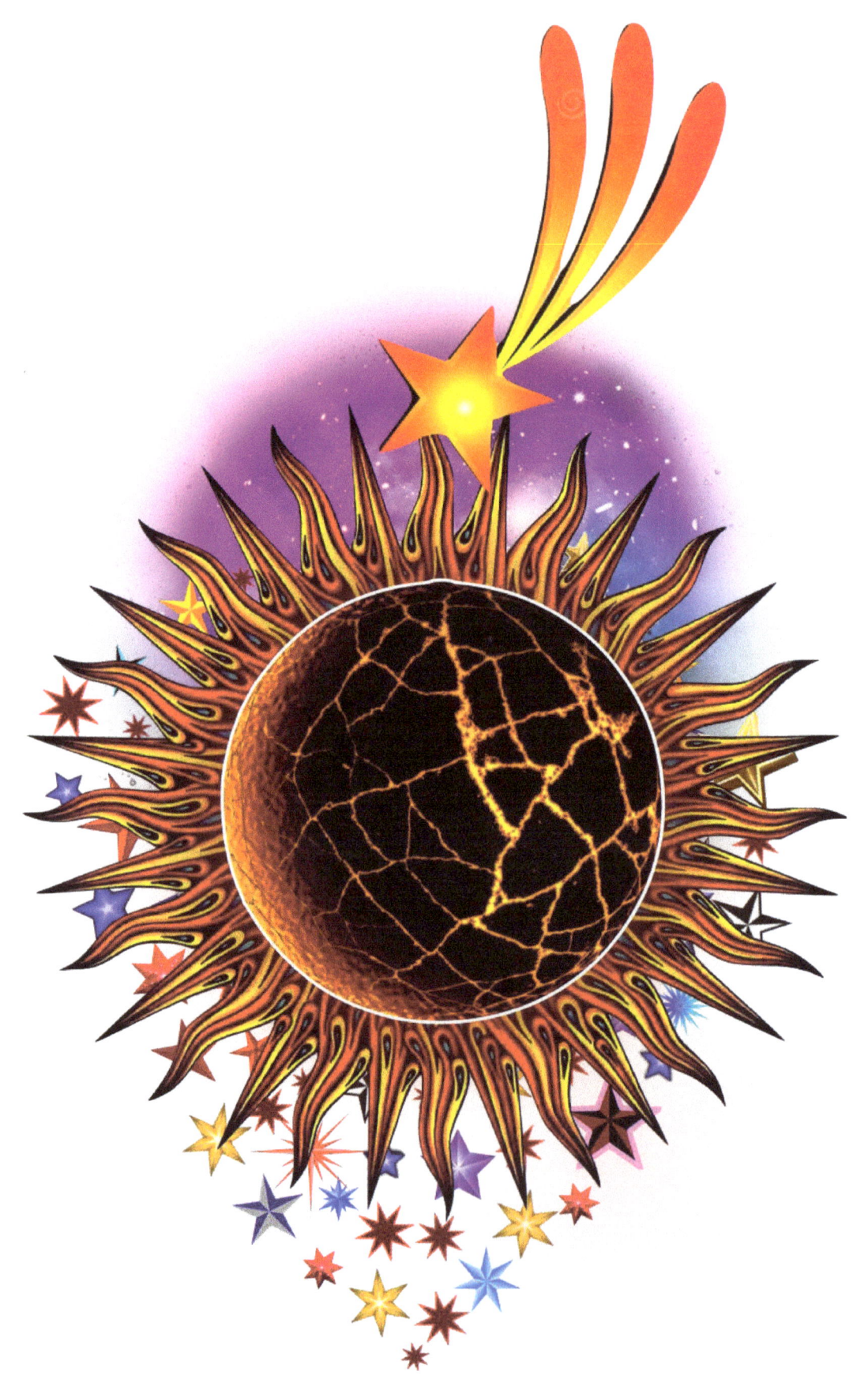

"I will shake the heavens, and the earth shall remove out of her place." (Isaiah 13:13).

Star light, star
bright, the first star I see
tonight. I wish I may, I wish I
might, have the wish
I wish tonight.

We cannot
predict the future
by plotting the position
of the stars, but we catch a
glimpse of our destiny
we see a stellar light
in the eyes of the
faithful.

When we look up at the heavens,
we see "torrents of light and rivers of the air,
along whose bed the glimmering stars are seen like
gold and silver sands in some ravine, where mountain
streams have left their channels bare." Heavenly Father
"descends in the sheen of His celestial armor, on serene
and quiet nights, when all the heavens are fair."
Stardust "is whirled aloft, and flies from
the invisible chariot wheels of God."
(Wordsworth, "The Galaxy").

"When evening makes
its quiet entrance across the skies,
out through the darkness that, quivering,
dies, beautiful, broad, and white, fashioned
of many a silver ray and stolen out of the
ruins of day, grows the pale bridge of
the Milky Way, built by the
Architect of night."
(Anon).

"All the host of heaven shall be dissolved, and the heavens shall be rolled together as a scroll." (Isaiah 34:4).

When we
look up at the stars,
we see fire-folk sitting in the
air, in bright boroughs and circled
citadels. (See Gerald Hopkins,
"The Starlight Night").

"I intend
to go not only
farther than any
man has been before
me, but as far as I
think it is possible
for a man to go."
(James Cook).

It
is the
night sky
that steals our
imaginations. The
stars in the heavens
whisper that the world
is full of limitless
possibilities.

A soft glow
coming from the
stars in the heavens
above may be our only
source of light as we
make our way back
home on a dark
and dreary
night.

"O Lord, thou art
our father, we are the clay,
and thou our potter, and we are
the work of thy hands."
(Isaiah 64:8).

"We have it in our power
to begin the world over again."
(Thomas Paine, 1776).

Each
time a baby
is born, the world
itself is born all
over again.

Isn't it
ironic that we
have emerged from
the dust of stars
to contemplate
the universe
around
us.

Everything
matters because
everything in the
universe is made
up of matter.

"Image
a world in
which nations
find the search for
life in the universe
more interesting than
taking life on earth."
(Neil Tyson).

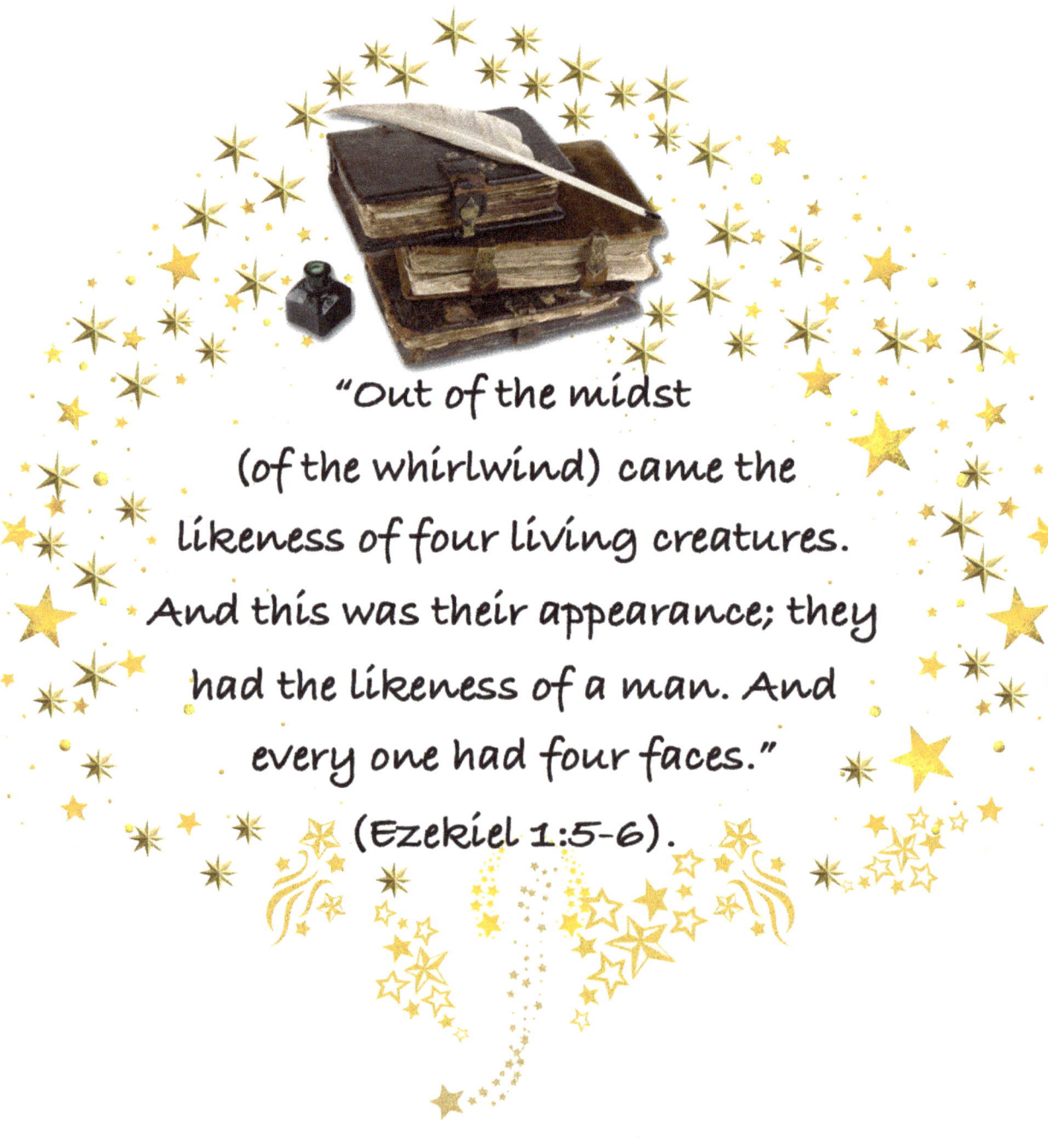

"Out of the midst (of the whirlwind) came the likeness of four living creatures. And this was their appearance; they had the likeness of a man. And every one had four faces."

(Ezekiel 1:5-6).

The Light of Christ exerts a
nurturing influence throughout the cosmos.
Although we must daily travel farther from the
East, we are nevertheless oriented toward the radiant
glow emanating from that distant horizon. It provides
us with the regularly recurring reassurance of a religious
recalibration that autocorrects with fortuitous frequency and
celestial precision. It envelops us in an intuitive appreciation
of where we came from, why we are here, and where we are
going. As in a heavenly language that is rhythmical,
melodious, soothing to our ears, and calming to
our souls, when we hear the Spirit quietly
whisper: "You're a stranger here," we
are comforted with the realization
that we have "wandered from
a more exalted sphere."

The Great Plan of Happiness
is all-inclusive. It was perfectly designed,
that there might be no strangers or foreigners in
the household of God. The Plan teaches that we must
focus our minds and our hearts on the heavens, so that
we might one day see that we are not just the citizens of a
community, state, nation, or world, but are active members
of a celestial Federation of Planets, or an interstellar union
of planetary nation-states that operates semi-autonomously
within God's heavenly theocracy. Our own stellar union will
be founded upon the principles of liberty, equality, progress,
and justice and peace, with the sole purpose of furthering the
universal potential of all sentient life in the galaxy. We will
be as gods in embryo, committed to the principles related to
improvement. We will share resources, encourage peaceful
cooperation, and strive to be faithfully obedient, as we
continue to participate in an exciting exploration
that probes the borders of the unknown
possibilities of existence.

"There is a God in heaven that revealeth secrets."
(Daniel 2:28).

What
we get by reaching
our destination is not nearly
as important as what we become by
reaching our destination. We are often
dissatisfied because we have traded what
we need for what we want. It is our character
that nudges us off our status quo, it is our
commitment that gets us moving, and it
is our discipline that keeps us on track
to boldly go where no one has ever
gone before; even to travel
among the stars.

The United
Federation of Planets
was a vast interstellar alliance
in the fictional Star Trek Universe.
It was committed to 1) saving succeeding
generations from the devastation of inter-stellar
war, 2) re-affirming faith in the rights of sentient
beings and in the dignity and worth of all life forms,
3) guaranteeing the equal rights of members of planetary
systems large and small, 4) establishing conditions under
which justice and mutual respect for the obligations arising
from treaties and other sources of interplanetary law might be
maintained, 5) promoting social progress and better standards
of living on all worlds, 6) practicing benevolent tolerance and
living together in peace with each other as good neighbors, 7)
uniting in strength, and maintaining interstellar peace
and security, 8) ensuring that armed force should not
be used, except for the common defense, and 9) for
the promotion of the advancement of all life
forms, utilizing all available
interstellar resources.

"How great are his signs! And how mighty are his wonders!" (Daniel 4:3).

We experience First Contact with Deity when God says: "Well done thou good and faithful servant ... enter thou into the joy of thy lord." (Matthew 25:21). As we do so, we become a "warp capable" civilization, and qualify by our obedience to eternally valid principles to join the exalted community of a United Federation of Planets under the heavens.

Heavenly Father gives us the Spirit as we are tested and allowed to demonstrate how we would think and act if entrusted with His power. We speak purposefully as did Nephi, who confirmed: "My God will give me, if I ask not amiss." (2 Nephi 4:35). Passing this verbal exam moves us to the head of the class, from Federation space right to the borders of Zion, where we are "encircled about with the matchless bounty of His love." (Alma 26:15).

Dancing With the Stars, the real question is: "As we exert ourselves on the mortal stage of the learning laboratory of life, is our performance of such significance that it will forever determine our status?" If we do not do so now, will we ever in the eternities to come be able to stand before a panel of celestial judges, having amended our behavior and having mastered the footwork of a quick step that promises to carry us all the way to the gates of heaven?

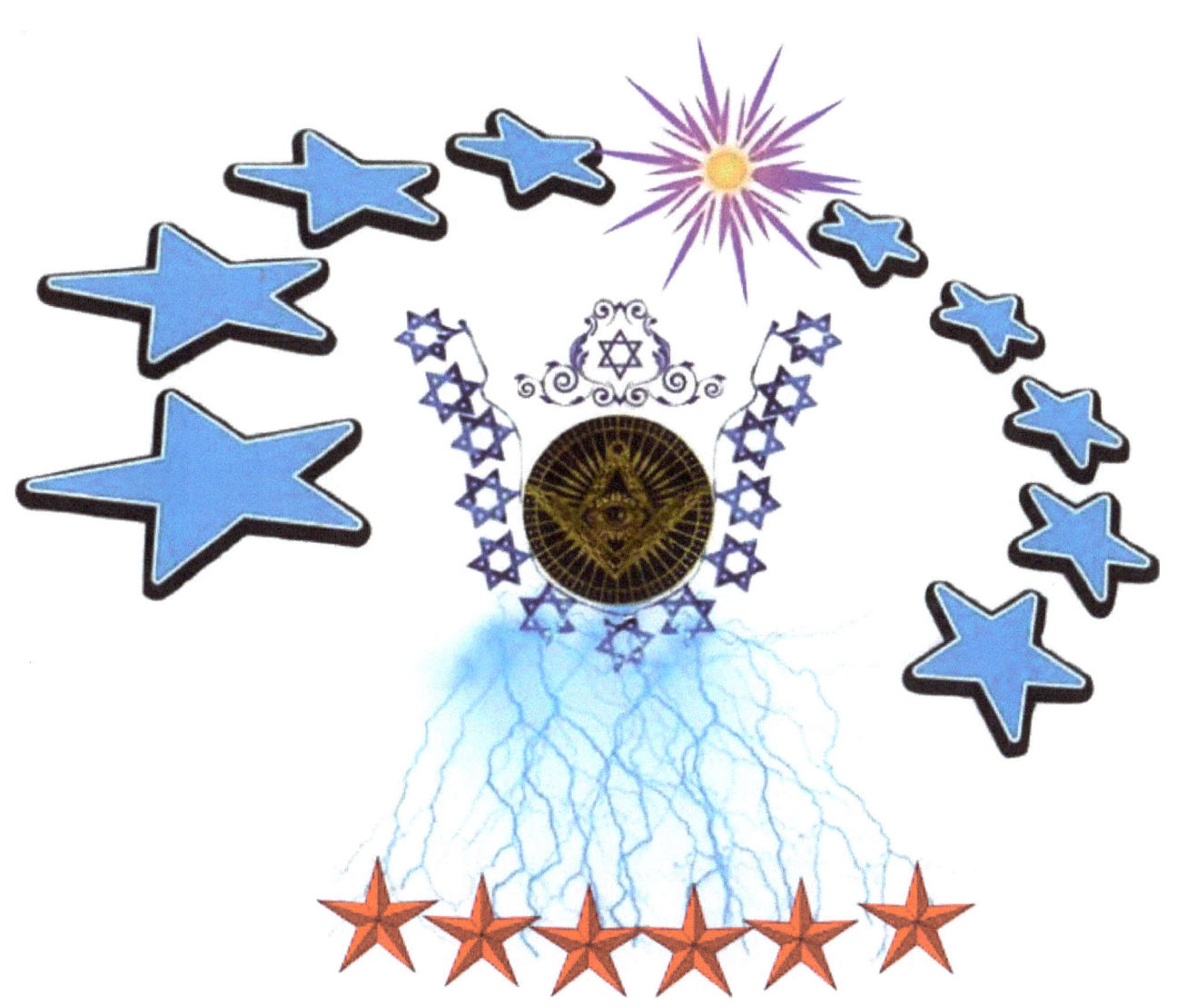

"His kingdom is an everlasting kingdom, and his dominion is from generation to generation." (Daniel 4:3).

Nothing of
consequence ever dies, for
the resurrection transforms
us and brings us into the
greater light of day.

"We all have
calcium in our bones and
iron in our veins. There is carbon in
our souls and nitrogen in our brains. We
are 98% stardust, and our spirits are made
of flames. We are all heavenly stars that
just happen to have people names."
(Nikita Gill).

The Author of Eternal
Salvation, Who is both the finisher of
our faith and the fashioner of worlds without end,
exhorts us to drink copiously and unceasingly from a
fountain of truth, thereby to slake our thirst for principles
that stabilize our lives and gyroscopically orient us toward
heaven. Only Gospel bedrock can provide the footing that is
needed to establish that equilibrium, supply the stability
we so desperately need in an uncertain world, help us to
steady the helm as we navigate treacherous waters, and
give each one of us the poise and composure of a truly
balanced life. This lesson of balance is one that, if
taken to heart, will kindle our faith, protect our
testimonies, and even save our souls. It will
help us to better understand our place in
the divine design that our Father in
Heaven followed when He created
the cosmos in which we live
and move, and have
our being.

"I saw … visions, and, behold, one like the Son of man came with the clouds of heaven." (Daniel 7:13).

We exercise our priesthood in meekness and humility, but in a way that reflects a righteous authority transcending that of Christopher Pike, James T. Kirk, Johnathon Archer, Jean-Luc Picard, Katherine Janeway, and Benjamin Cisco. It is patterned after the might, majesty, power, and dominion of our Heavenly Commander, Who is the leader of a galactic federation and celestial theocracy.

We take it on God's word that there is sentient life out there in the far reaches of the cosmos. For all we know, our Creator may count as His children those who live on Cardassia Prime, as well as on the Romulan Home World. But it is unlikely that His children on Vulcan have pointed ears. There may be teeming populations on Ferenginar, but it is doubtful that they are governed by 285 Rules of Acquisition. If there are Klingons, whether they rule an empire or wield the Bat'leth is debatable.

Just as the power of ultraviolet light is used in sterilization, (ultraviolet germicidal irradiation), the manifestation of the unearthly light that radiates from the presence of God purifies and renews us. "Though your sins be as scarlet," Isaiah promised, "they shall be as white as snow; though they be red like crimson, they shall be as wool."
(Isaiah 1:18)

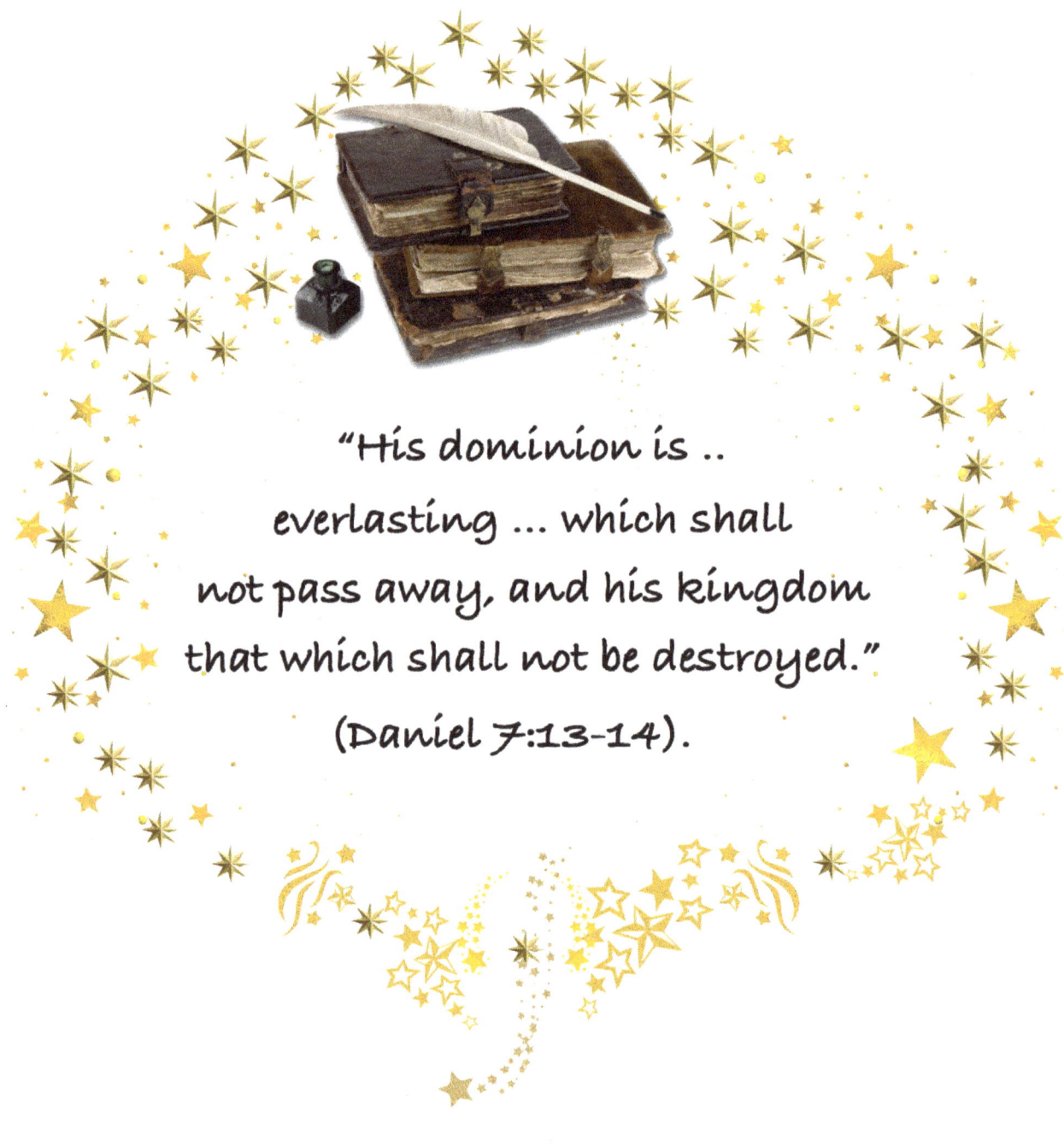

"His dominion is ..
everlasting ... which shall
not pass away, and his kingdom
that which shall not be destroyed."
(Daniel 7:13-14).

Art mimics life,
and life mimics eternity.

After all is said and
done, when all the leaders
of the Church have been quoted
and the relevant scriptures have been
cited, the fact remains that we have not been
given the revelation that answers the questions
that relate to the possibility of the progression of
God's children between kingdoms of glory after
the Resurrection. But intuitively we all want to
believe that God's grace is so great, and is so
powerful, that it is sufficient for us to do
so. For saints and sinners alike, the
power of the Atonement must be
both infinite and eternal.

In a grand exposition,
Lehi declared that all things
have their opposite. (See 2 Nephi 2:11).
In addition to the familiar applications of this
basic principle, Lehi may have also meant that our
world has an isomer. (An isomer may be thought of as
one of two or more compounds, radicals, or ions that contain
the same number of atoms of the same elements but differ in
structural arrangement and properties.) What if the world as
we know it has one specific molecular formula, but the world
we cannot see, that is its mirror, has a different isomeric
structural formula? Could Lehi have also been saying
that our world is "without beginning of days or
end of years, being prepared from eternity to
all eternity, according to" our Father
in Heaven's "foreknowledge" of
all things? (Alma 13:7).

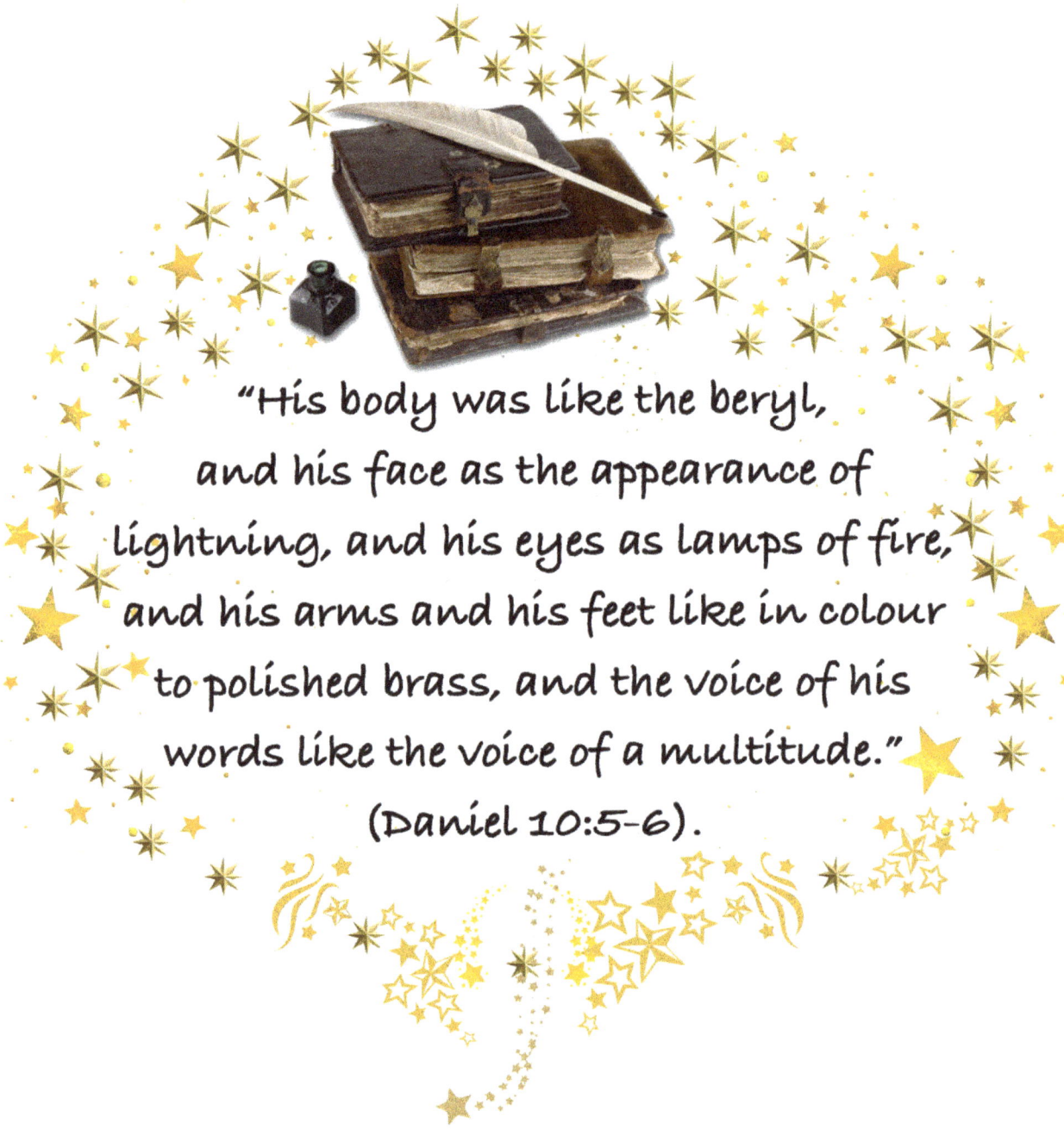

"His body was like the beryl, and his face as the appearance of lightning, and his eyes as lamps of fire, and his arms and his feet like in colour to polished brass, and the voice of his words like the voice of a multitude." (Daniel 10:5-6).

We can
know our
Savior on the
terms that He has
established, or we will
know Him not at all.

Our comprehension of the
universe is at risk when we set
our sights too low and we side-step
into conceptual cul-de-sacs from which
there are few retreats. Certainly, those with
only a three-dimensional view of the world
will see things not as they really are, but
only as their limited understanding
permits them to see. The inherent
danger is: "Where there is no
vision, the people perish."
(Proverbs 29:18).

What are the temporal and spatial
bounds of the heavens or the seas, or of the
dry land, or of the sun, moon, or stars? For all
practical purposes, we live in a three-dimensional
world and move thru time in a forward direction at
the rate of one day every 24 hours. We can be certain
that these bounds will continue to be mathematically
defined with greater and greater precision, even as they
are esoterically debated by theologians and philosophers
alike. But what about heaven? We have the assurance
that the relationship between finite boundaries
and the thrones, dominions, principalities,
and powers that relate to the eternal
worlds will be revealed, as well.
(See Colossians 1:16).

"The Lord God will do nothing, but he revealeth his secret unto his servants the prophets." (Amos 3:7).

When we find ourselves thinking rationally, we are constrained by the very things from which we yearn to be free: our mortal perspective and perceptions. These are the sum and substance of our temporal experience. We seek the right answers, but too often ask the wrong questions. Our efforts to construct a viable definition of heaven and earth by subtraction, rather than by addition, are doomed to failure. God's reality is infinitely richer and much more satisfying than a rational approach grudgingly concedes could possibly exist. It is more than we could ever hope to understand were we to rely only upon the poor and corruptible lenses of our bodies.

Perhaps the agnostic Greeks of Paul's day were not far from the mark when they erected "an altar with this inscription: To the Unknown God." (Acts 17:23). Only a Gospel perspective can help us to discover His roles as both the Guardian of the Galaxy and the Master of Creation.

The Gospel endows us with a multi-dimensional perspective on existence that provides a much more accurate context in which to develop a construct of the universe in which we live. In this sense, "the glory of God is intelligence" with the ability to distinguish between the physical and spiritual worlds around us, even the multi-dimensional worlds that we cannot see with our eyes.

"I will utter things which have been kept secret from the foundation of the world." (Matthew 13:35).

Adjacent
layered dimensional
realities may have been the focus
of Abraham's vision, when the Lord
"put his hand upon (the patriarch's) eyes,
and (he) saw those things which (God's)
hands had made, which were many, and
they multiplied before (his) eyes, and
(he) could not see the end thereof."
(Abraham 3:12).

Mormon explained: "The day soon
cometh that your mortal must put on
immortality, and these bodies which are
now moldering in corruption must
soon become incorruptible bodies."
(Mormon 6:21). Maybe it has
always been a question of
dimension, rather than
of time and place.

In heaven, there are "celestial
bodies, and bodies terrestrial: but the
glory of the celestial is one, and the glory
of the terrestrial is another. There is one glory of
the sun, and another glory of the moon, and another
glory of the stars: for one star differeth from another
in glory. So, also, is the resurrection of the dead …
It is sown a natural body; it is raised a spiritual
body." (1 Corinthians 15:40-44). Nothing of
consequence ever dies, for the resurrection
transforms us and brings us into the
greater light of a day that promises
to be brighter than even the most
spectacular supernova
could ever be.

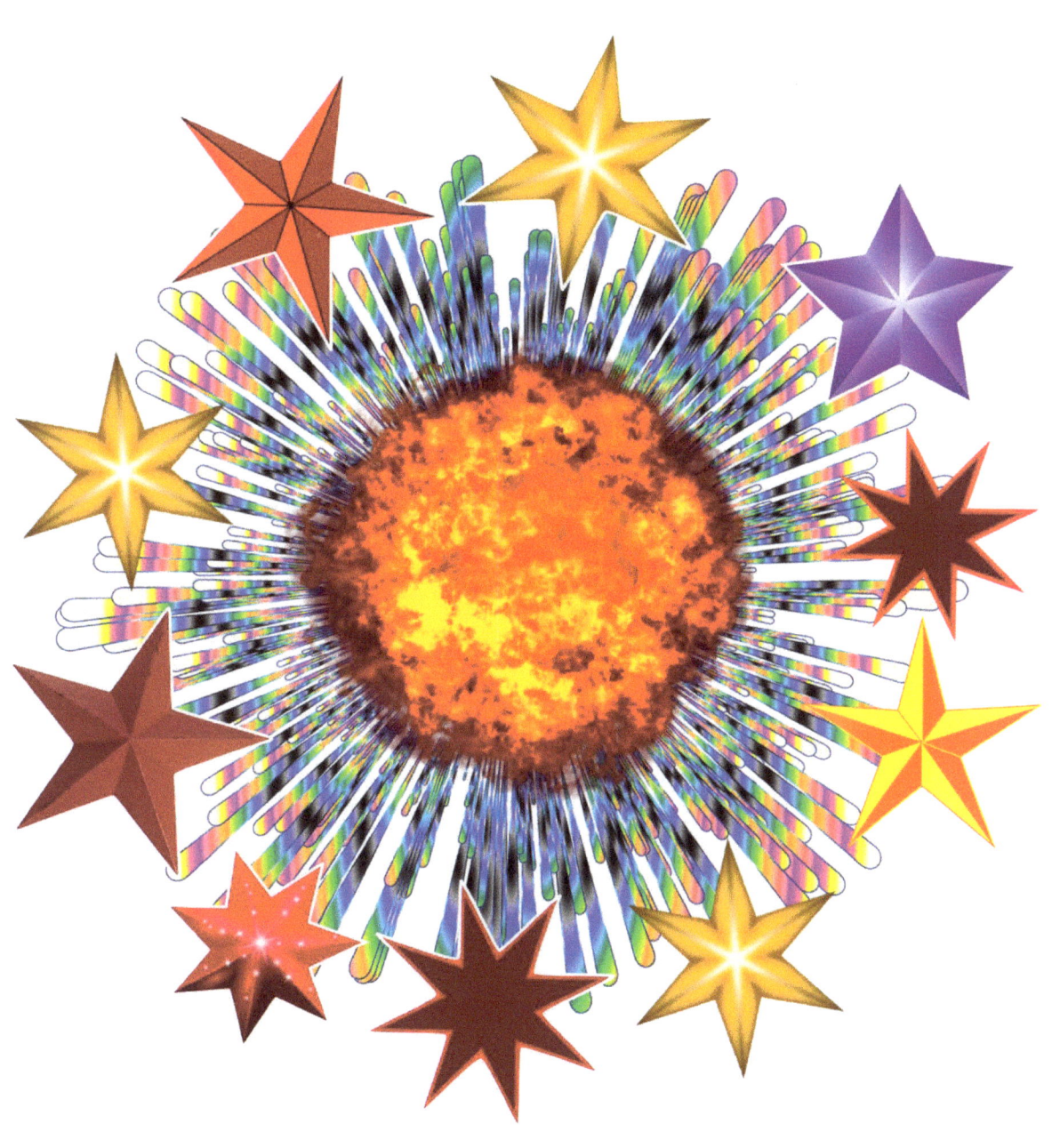

"All things were made by him, and without him was not anythig made that was made." (John 1:3).

How do God and angels move about His creations without continually violating the laws of physics? Even at light speed, it would take over ninety billion years to traverse the known universe, so physically traveling within three-dimensional space and one-dimensional time seems to be unlikely. It has been our experience that as soon as we have captured the attention of God, His intercession in our behalf can be instantaneous, no matter where in His creations He may have been previously engaged.

Visiting "other sheep" may be a cognitively comfortable way of describing how God might travel between dimensions. Similarly, Alma might have been speaking literally when he explained that there is a space between death and the resurrection. (See Alma 40:9).

It may be the easy access by our Father in Heaven to the higher dimensions of eternity that facilitates our own 'restoration'. From the vantage point of the heavens, as He looks down on all the seraphic host, not by going to the left, or to the right, and not by going forward or backward, or up or down, but by simultaneously going at right angles to every one of those directions, God is in an ideal position to bring to pass our immortality and eternal life.

"Verily I say unto you, Hereafter, ye shall see heaven open, and the angels of God ascending and descending."

(John 1:51).

It was while he was under the spell of the mighty influence of the Spirit that Moses beheld "many lands, and each land was called earth, and there were inhabitants on the face thereof." What if these earths were in parallel dimensions? Could they have been temporal and spatial worlds that were stacked on top of each other like the pages between the covers of a book? Then, the Lord told Moses: "Worlds without number have I created … for behold, there are many worlds that have passed away by the word of my power. And there are many that now stand, and innumerable are they unto man; but all things are numbered unto me, for they are mine and I know them." (Moses 1:29, 33 & 35).

An interaction between parallel universes took place when "the glory of God was upon Moses, therefore, Moses could endure his presence" to better appreciate and experience His eternal perspective. With this preparation, he was commanded: "Look, and I will show thee the workmanship of mine hands." At the same time, however, the Lord said: "My works are without end, and also my words, for they never cease. Wherefore, no man can behold all my works, except he behold all my glory." Then, He revealed: "All things are present with me, for I know them all." (Moses 1:2-6). But Moses needed to receive the spiritual element characterized by God as His glory, that he might be aware of all things, and that he might experience them as his present reality

"The Spirit itself beareth witness with our spirit, that we are the children of God." (Romans 8:16).

"You just don't get it, do you, Jean-Luc?" asked Q, of the captain of the Starship Enterprise. "The trial never ends. We wanted to see f you had the ability to expand your mind to new horizons, and for one brief moment, you did. For that one fraction of a second, you were open to options you had never considered. That is the exploration that awaits you. Not mapping stars and studying nebula, but charting the unknown possibilities of existence."

The Gospel Plan has been ordained by God to ease our transition from the world of every day into eternity, where the eyes of our understanding will be opened, and we will be reintroduced to the society of celestial beings who have embraced their ongoing mission to bring about the immortality and eternal life of star children just like us, across the galaxy. The total power of the sunlight that strikes the atmosphere of Earth each day is 174 petawatts. In eternity, however, we will be Dancing with Stars Who utilize the power of the untold billions of petawatts that energize the celestial world lying somewhere beyond the borders of the final frontiers of space and time. It was ordained in the heavens, that, across the cosmos, we and our distant cousins might tap into that heavenly power and feel its influence as it helps us to deal with both adversity and the adversary, for all those in His creations "are alike unto God." (2 Nephi 26:33).

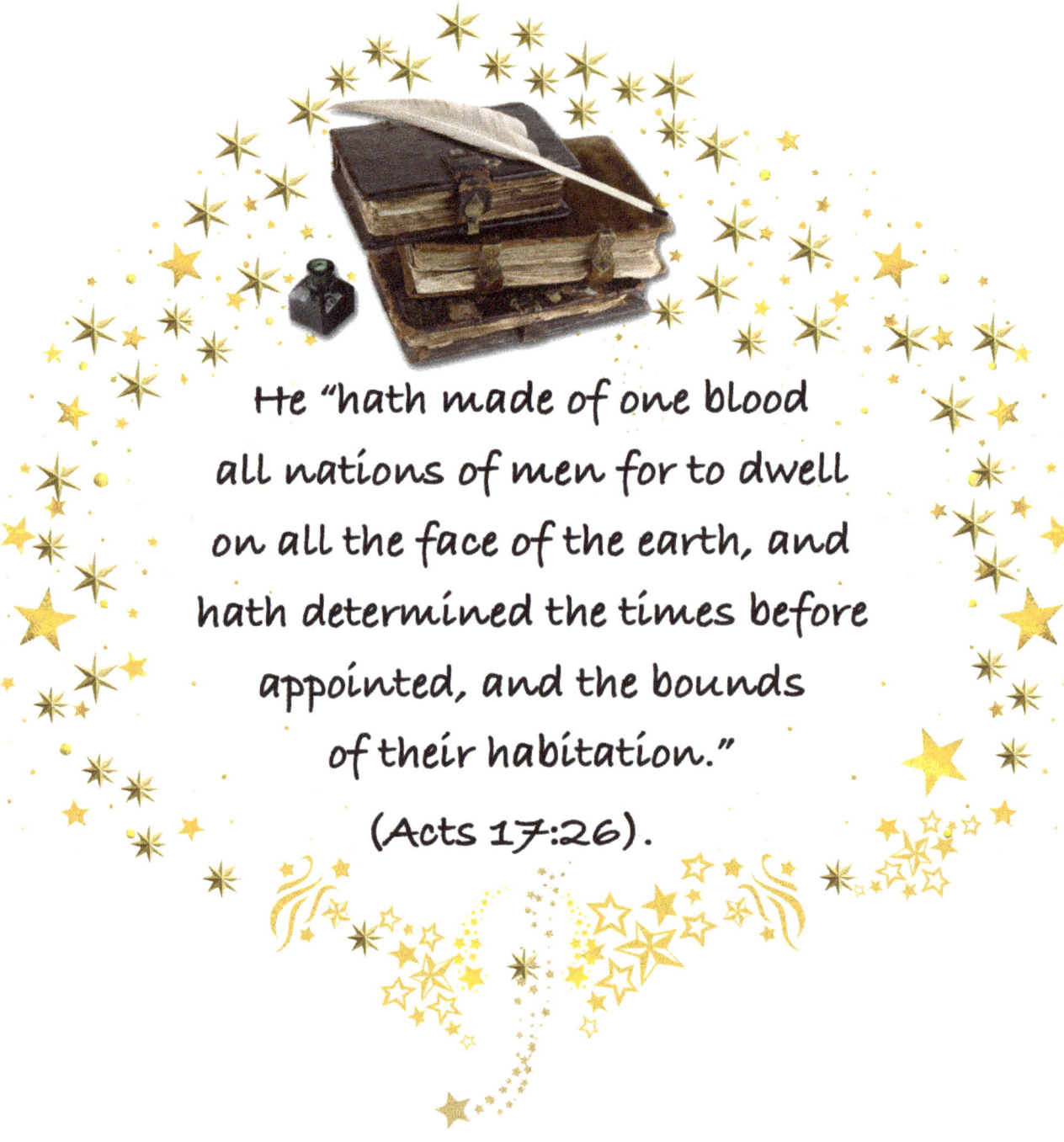

He "hath made of one blood all nations of men for to dwell on all the face of the earth, and hath determined the times before appointed, and the bounds of their habitation."

(Acts 17:26).

"When I consider the heavens," wrote David, "the work of thy fingers, the moon, and the stars, which thou hast ordained; What is man, that thou art mindful of him? And the son of man, that thou visitest him? For thou hast made him a little lower than the angels." (Psalms 8:3-5). Perhaps the natural abode of the angels is within a higher dimensional reality. If so, the work of His fingers, even the moon, and the stars, might have been ordained by Heavenly Father to exist in worlds that are beyond our comprehension.

For now, our poor lenses cannot discern what is really there. "No man hath seen God at any time in the flesh, except quickened by the Spirit of God?" (J.S.T. John 1:18). If it is true that "the light of the body is the eye," then, when the eye is single to faith, our "whole body shall be full of light." (3 Nephi 13:22).

Elder Orson Pratt appreciated the ramifications of the doctrine that celestial beings can perceive with all parts of their bodies. "The spirit," he said, "is inherently capable of experiencing the sensations of light. I think we could then see in different directions at once. Instead of looking in one direction, we could then look all around us at the same instant."

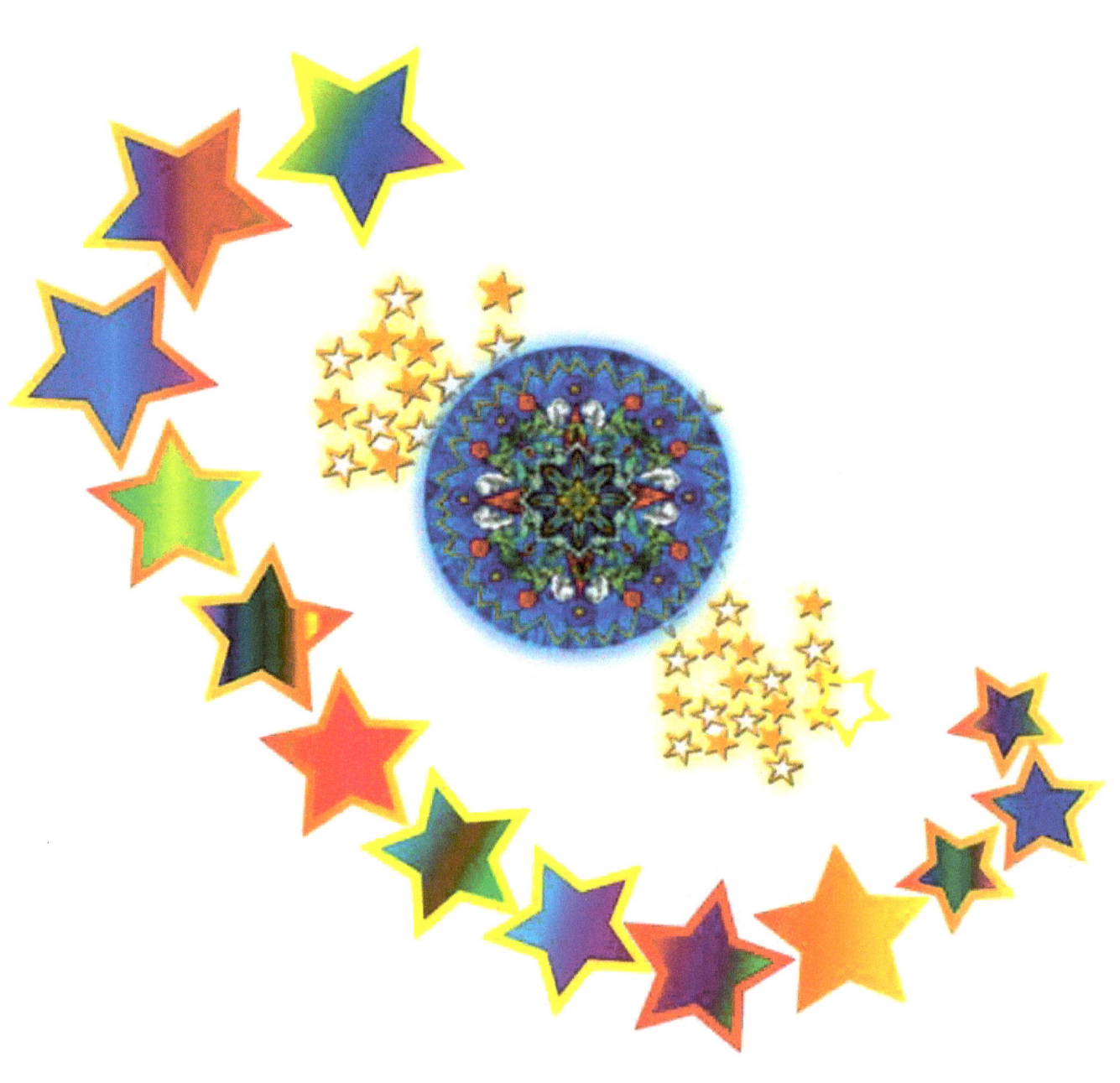

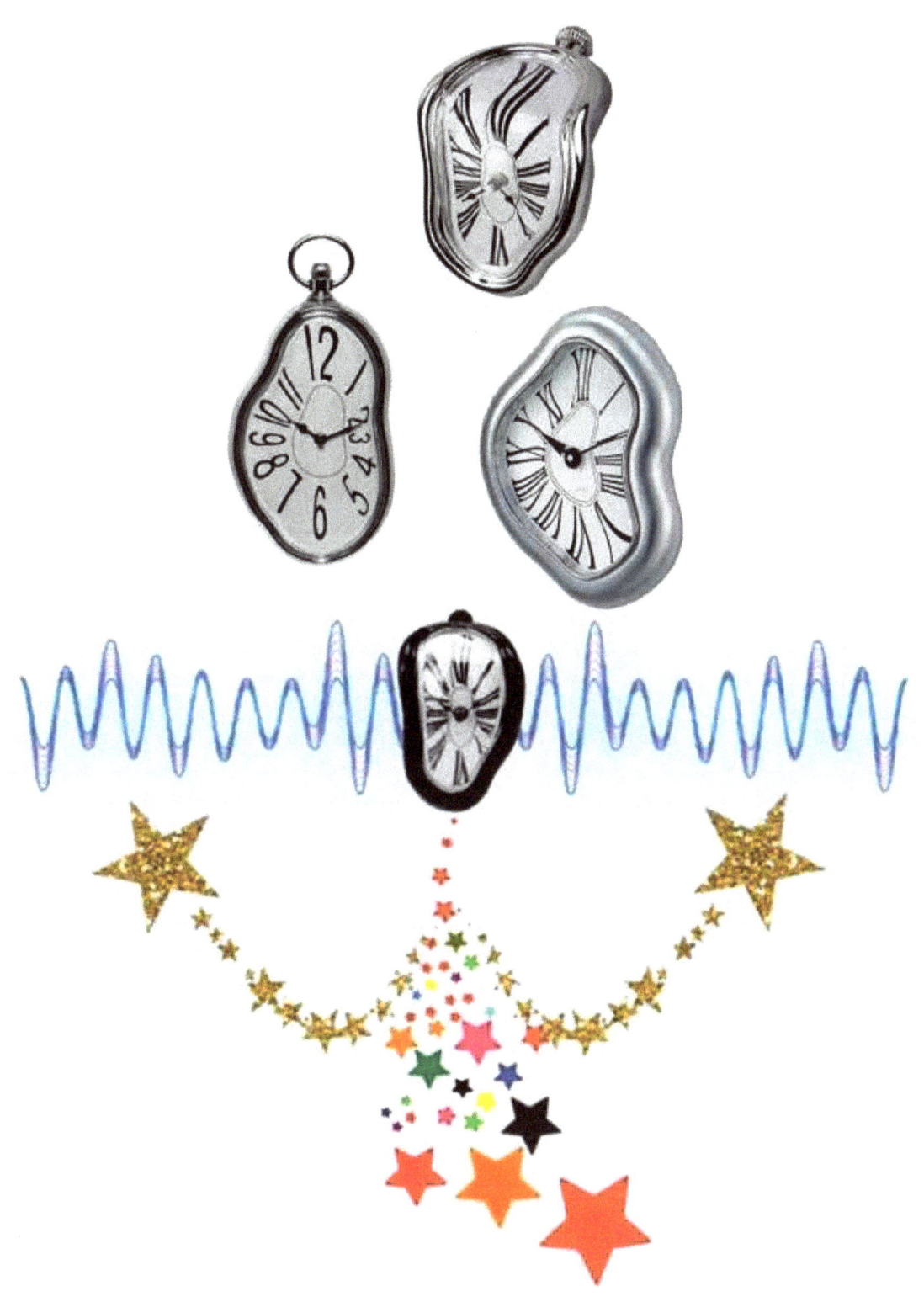

"Unto him be glory in the church by Christ Jesus throughout all ages, world without end." (Ephesians 3:21).

After a heavenly messenger announced to shepherds tending their flocks by night in the fields near Bethlehem that Christ the Lord had been born, "suddenly there was with the angel a multitude of the heavenly host praising God." (Luke 2:13). A dramatic manifestation of beings from the unseen world prompted the shepherds to hurry to Bethlehem to see the things that had come to pass, that the Lord had made known unto them. (Luke 2:15).

Wherever, whenever, or however we might ultimately fit into the divine design of heaven and the grand scheme of the cosmos, we do know this for a surety: God quickens life in the sense that He has provided our spirits with an animated physical world with which we freely interact; He "lends (us) breath, that (we) may live and move and do according to (our) own will, and (He supports us) from one moment to another." (Mosiah 2:21).

Our Pale Blue Dot and everything on it are only shadows of things to come, but we must not expect our understanding to approach the level of the comprehension of God. Truly, did Paul observe: "For now we see through a glass, darkly, but then face to face. Now I know in part; but then shall I know even as also I am known." (1 Corinthians 13:12).

"I saw a new heaven and a new earth, for the first heaven and the first earth were passed away, and there was no more sea." (Revelation 21:1).

Perhaps
only millennial
beings will have the power to
transition back and forth from
the mortal world to realms that are
dimensionally superior, for they
will live in a state that bears
striking similarities
to translation.

Throughout the
Millennium, the relationship
between the Earth and the eternal
worlds may be so well-defined and
stabilized that transitions between
the two will be more frequently,
predictably, and easily
accomplished.

When we achieve
the state of refinement that
is envisioned by the Merciful Plan
of The Great Creator, we will then be able
to understand what the Dead Sea Covenanter
meant when he wrote: "For mine own part, I have
reached the intervision, and thru the Spirit Thou
hast placed within me, I have come to know Thee,
my God." Perhaps, the "intervision" describes a
state of consciousness that enables us to see
all the way from Earth right into heaven,
and even into the furthest reaches of
the eternal mansions that have
been prepared for us by our
Heavenly Father.

"God spake unto Moses, saying: Behold, I am the Lord God Almighty, and Endless is my name; for I am without beginning of days or end of years." (Moses 1:3).

Among
all of God's creations,
just how many stars must
continually be born, to help Him
bring to pass His work and glory?
One can only guess, but consider this:
There are 600 billion galaxies in the known
universe, and, within each one, three stars are
born per year. At the same time, one star "dies"
per year. But to be on the conservative side, let's
assume that 1 star per year, and not 2, is added
to the inventory of celestial objects within a
typical galaxy. Therefore, the cumulative
number of stars born every year in the
universe might easily be six hundred
billion: 1 new star each year, in
each galaxy. That is roughly
1.6 billion new stars on
any given day, or
18,500 stars per
second.

In the past
413 years, ever since
Galileo Galilei heard about
the "Danish perspective glass"
in 1609, and looked up at the stars
through the primitive telescope that he
built according to its specifications, over
247,200,000,000,000 stars have been born.
Our Creator fashioned our universe, worlds
without end, in accordance with a Divine
Design. Our galaxy is a star nursery,
a pediatric intensive care unit for
protostars, and a neonatal
stellar incubator.

"Moses beheld the world and the ends thereof, and all the children of men which are, and which were created."

(Moses 1:8).

When you
go to bed tonight
under a waxing moon
and a starlit sky, by the time
you wake up in the morning after
a refreshing eight hours of sleep, (which
is eight hours of active labor in the birthing
center of the universe), another five hundred
forty-eight million stars will have been born.
(547,945,205, to be exact – that's over half a
billion stars!) We can scarcely keep up, but
suffice to say: We should take the Lord at
His word when He assured us that
He has created worlds without
number.

"I am
a Child of God"
is a very good choice
of words when describing
the intimacy that our Heavenly
Father desires to have with us,
and with His children
everywhere.

The Prophet Joseph Smith
described the hierarchy that exists in
the heavens: "My Father worked out his kingdom
with fear and trembling, and I must do the same; and
when I get my kingdom, I shall present it to my Father, so
that he may obtain kingdom upon kingdom, and it will
exalt him in glory. He will then take a higher exaltation,
and I will take his place, and thereby become exalted
myself. Jesus treads in the tracks of the Father,
and inherits what God did before."

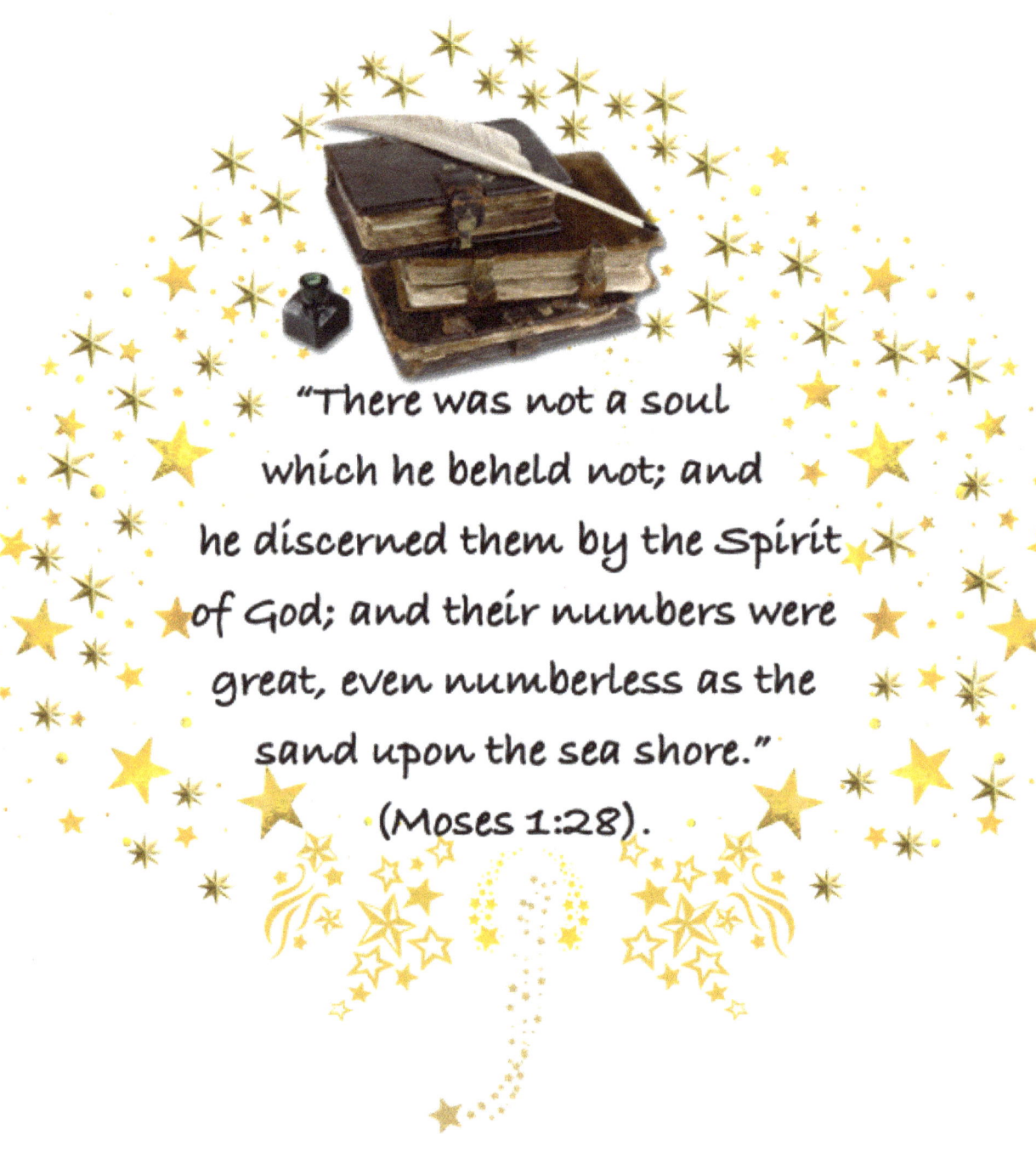

"There was not a soul which he beheld not; and he discerned them by the Spirit of God; and their numbers were great, even numberless as the sand upon the sea shore." (Moses 1:28).

It is from Kolob, nearest to the celestial, or the residence of God, that the order of creation is temporally and spatially governed, and it is from there that the boundaries of heaven are established in such a manner that it is beyond the reach of detection by even the most sophisticated and delicately calibrated instruments that are utilized by terrestrial scientists.

The day may come when we summon others of God's children who live upon the shores of distant isles in a vast cosmic ocean, to come in out of the cold depth of space to enjoy the warm inviting companionship of the way, the truth, the life, and the light of worlds without end.

The veil functions as an event horizon that denies our senses any suggestion of what lies beyond. Only the Spirit has the power to penetrate the barrier that isolates us from the sum of eternal reality. Only the Spirit will answer our queries that plumb the depths of eternity: "O God, where art thou? And where is the pavilion that covereth thy hiding place? (D&C 121:1).

"Worlds without number have I created." (Moses 1:33).

If you hold up
a grain of sand at
arm's length against the
night sky, hidden behind
the blocked-out area there
are 2,000 galaxies, each
of which contains 100
billion to 1 trillion
or more stars.

The celestial world is an open
system. It is independent of spacetime. God
belongs to eternity, and so He carries out His
activities within the parameters of celestial laws
that build upon, supersede, or simply do not apply
to the laws that govern our physical universe. Paul
explained to the Corinthian Saints: "The natural
man receiveth not the things of the Spirit of
God: for they are foolishness unto him;
neither can he know them, because
they are spiritually discerned."
(1 Corinthians 2:14).

Obedience to celestial laws allows
us to more easily "see and understand
the things of God, even those things which
were from the beginning, before the world was."
(D&C 76:12-13). Reconciliation with God allows
us to escape the limitations of our mortal clay as our
minds transcend the temporally unalterable laws of
physics, grapple with the spatially expansive laws
of heaven, and finally expand in a union
with the eternal principles that govern
His Celestial kingdom.

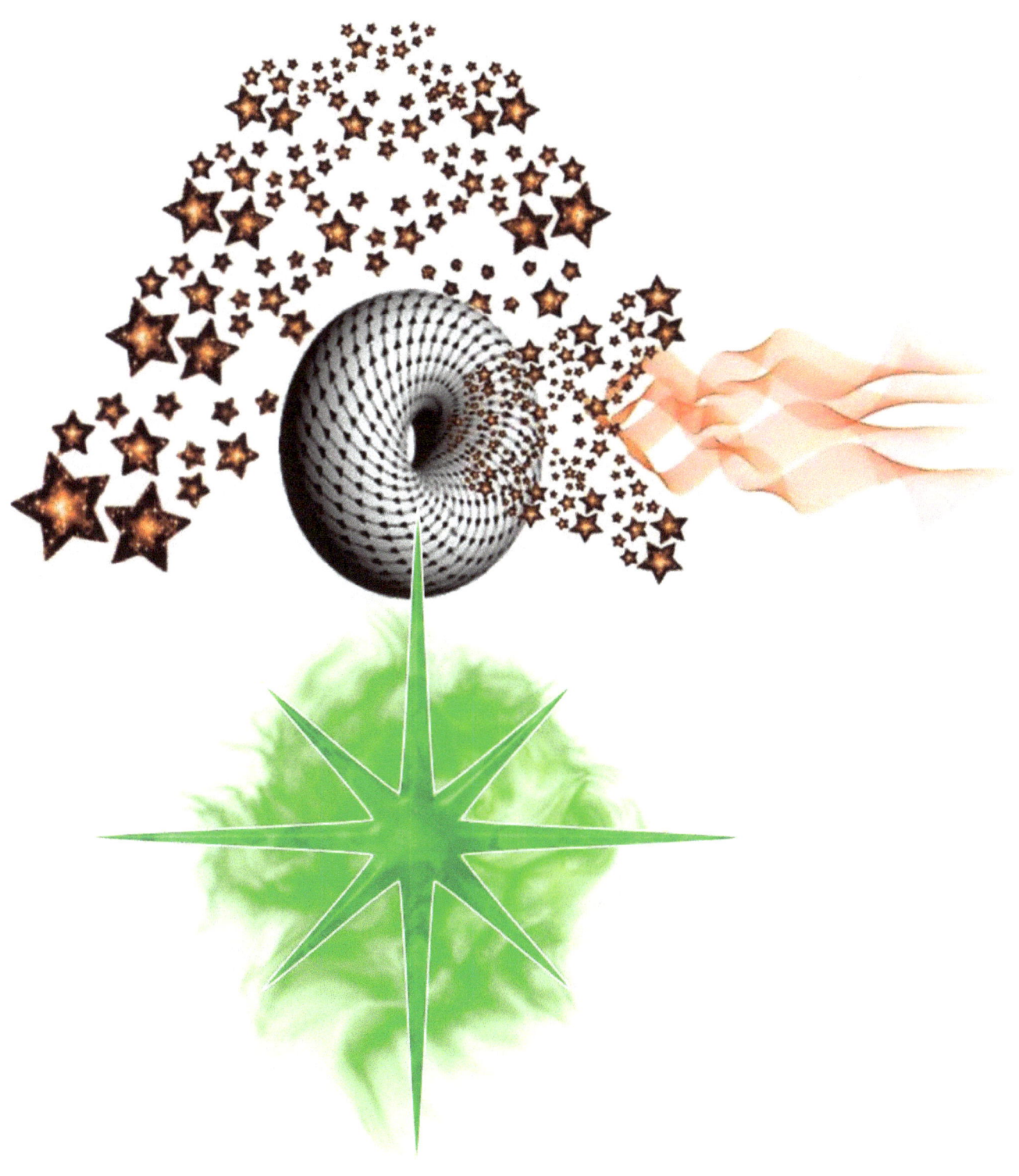

"The Lord God spake unto Moses, saying: The heavens, they are many, and they cannot be numbered unto man; but they are numbered unto me, for they are mine."
(Moses 1:37).

Does God obey the cosmic speed limit?" After all, yesterday, today, and forever are ever before Him in one eternal round, and He is "the Great I AM, Alpha and Omega, the beginning and the end, and the same which looked upon the wide expanse of eternity, and all the seraphic hosts of heaven before the world was made."
(D&C 38:1-2).

As the arrow of time flies into eternity, ostensibly straight and true, will it travel in two (or even multiple) directions, forward and backward, at once and forever? If it does so, will the bonds of its spatial limitations and temporal constraints be broken, that seem to be etched in stone at exactly 186,282.3969 miles per second?

After the Saints of God have been resurrected to celestial glory, their progression might shift its emphasis to their advancement to a dimensionally higher state of being as soon as they have prepared themselves to take that leap. In that case, they might eventually progress to have dominion over an infinite number of dimensionally inferior realms similar to their previous habitations. This might then allow those under their stewardship to advance to the position they had formerly occupied.

"I, the Lord God, had created all the children of men ... for in heaven created I them." (Moses 3:5).

To the prepared mind,
the Lord "will shew wonders
in the heavens and in the earth,
blood, and fire, and pillars of smoke."
(Joel 2:30).

When
time is no longer
an element of the equations
that define our existence, by an
act of God's Celestial Congress the
speed limit will be effectively repealed,
because the reality to which it had been
anchored will have been superseded
by the mathematics of eternity. In
that land without time, there will
be no speed limit, for the laws
of physics will have lost
all relevance.

Gradually, it will dawn on
us that Gospel principles relating
to the eternities just might supersede
the physical laws relating to the temporal
world. Those who have been "born of him" are
oriented to the expansive covenants of the eternal
world rather than the restrictive laws of terrestrial
spheres. "Whatsoever is born of God overcometh the
world" and is therefore free of the confinements
of the equations of mathematics and the
limitations of the laws of physics, in
an inexplicable, indescribable,
and yet undeniable way.
(1 John 5:3).

"He beheld the spirits that God had created." (Moses 6:36).

As Alma
explained to Corianton:
"All is as one day with God,
and time only is measured
unto men." (Alma 40:8).
Einstein was right.
Time is relative.

The veil is almost
transparent in our lives when
our spiritual sensitivity prepares
us to act. As our powers expand, we
experience the glittering facets of
the life of the Spirit. We find
ourselves Dancing With
the Stars.

If we were to
substitute the term
"Creation" for "Big Bang"
and ask where and when it took
place, the answer is everywhere and
forever. No one can say if God utilized
the laws of physics as we understand them
during the Creation, but what we do know is
that "by him, were all things created, that are in
heaven, and that are in earth, visible and invisible,
whether they be thrones, or dominions, or principalities,
or powers." (Colossians 1:16). This leaves the door ajar for
theologians to confidently debate science from a position
of strength, and it even goes a step beyond Intelligent
Design, because it boldly testifies that God Himself
guided the Creation. It was not a dispassionate
interaction between quarks, bosons,
fermions, and leptons.

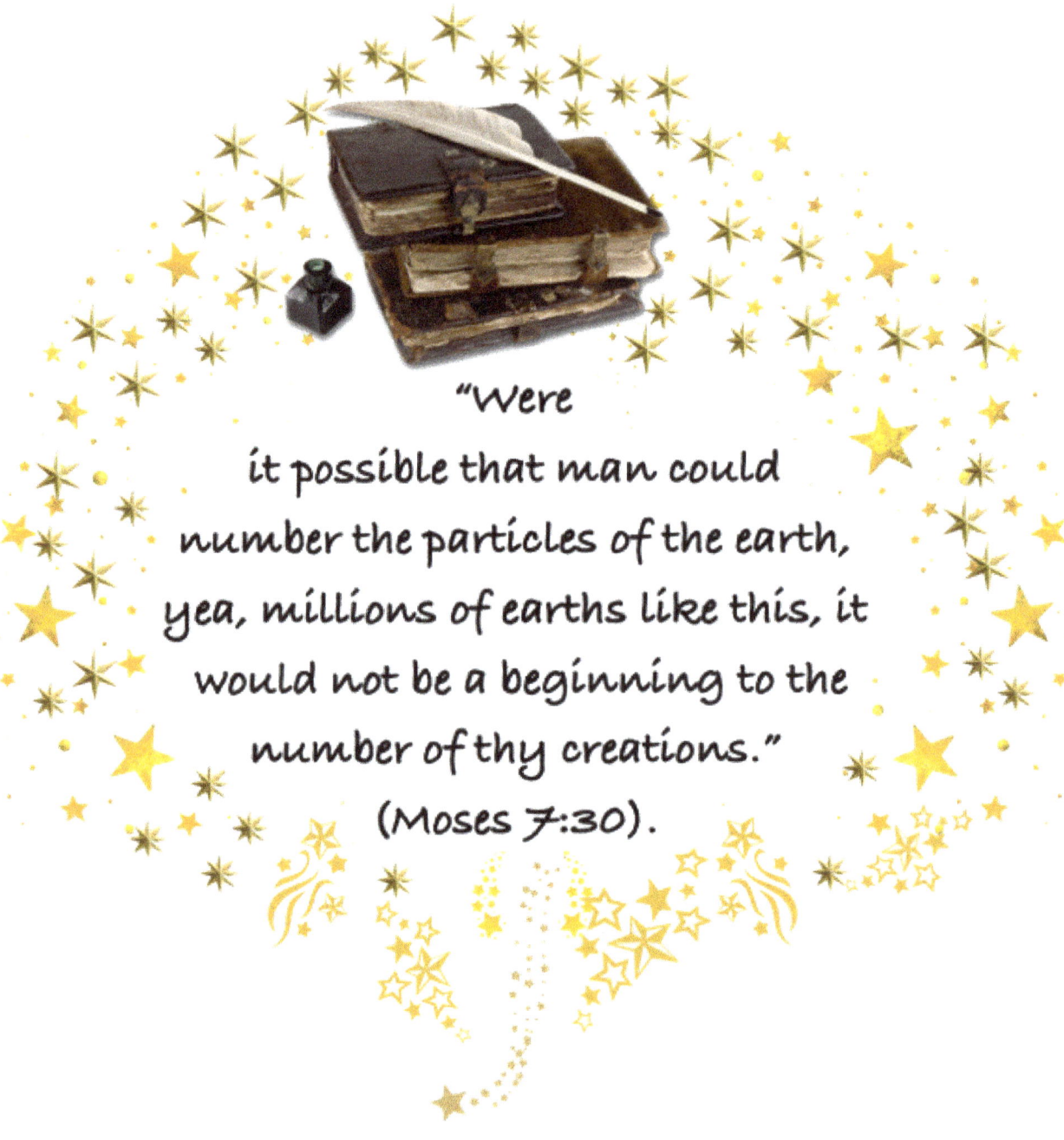

"Were it possible that man could number the particles of the earth, yea, millions of earths like this, it would not be a beginning to the number of thy creations."
(Moses 7:30).

Our destiny
was prepared for us in
the pre-earth existence. It is
molded in mortality, and will
be established in eternity, where the
heavens will benevolently smile upon us.
We will be immersed in the matchless glory
of immortality and eternal life, with thrones,
dominions, principalities, and powers, in an
endless hierarchy of kingdoms that renders
coherent the Savior's promise that in the
household of God there are many
mansions. (See John 14:2).

When
we look in a
mirror, we see the
glittering reflection
of a star-child.

When we have finally discovered the
castle of enchantment behind the hills of time,
we will find that growing "older" at the rate of one day
every twenty-four hours had been strictly and uniquely
a quality of mortality and a brilliant mechanism designed
by Heavenly Father to afford us an opportunity to gauge the
approach of our reunion with Him in the eternal world. We
will discover that we lived out our lives in only one dimly
lighted corner of reality. Thus, it was difficult for us to
appreciate our potential and grasp the power of our
position, that we might one day "flourish in
immortal youth, unhurt amidst the war
of elements, the wreck of matter,
and the crash of worlds."
(Joseph Addison).

"I can stretch forth mine hands and hold all the creations which I have made; and mine eye can pierce them also."
(Moses 7:36).

We have
all probably been
witnesses to interstellar
travel without having realized
it. Even now, there may be those
who walk among us who are not of
this world. We may frequently brush
shoulders with heavenly beings, for as
Paul forthrightly counseled the Saints:
"Be not forgetful to entertain strangers;
for thereby some have entertained
angels unawares." (Hebrews
13:2).

Whether or not it is clear to us,
the universe, and our lives, are
unfolding as they should.

Time is the medium within
which we live, and move, and have
our being. (See Acts 17:28). But, for most
of us, despite our impatience with its passage, we
are not yet prepared for the arrow of time to move up
and down, or side to side, let alone either forward or
backward. From a mortal perspective, time continues
to flow sluggishly, with the frustrating consistency
of cold molasses. To warm it up and get our juices
flowing, God injected covenants into its matrix
so that we might have the tools we would need
to live now, as well as in eternity. These
teach us how to create heaven on earth
as we retain a hope of eternal life
and engage mortality thru
the passage of time.

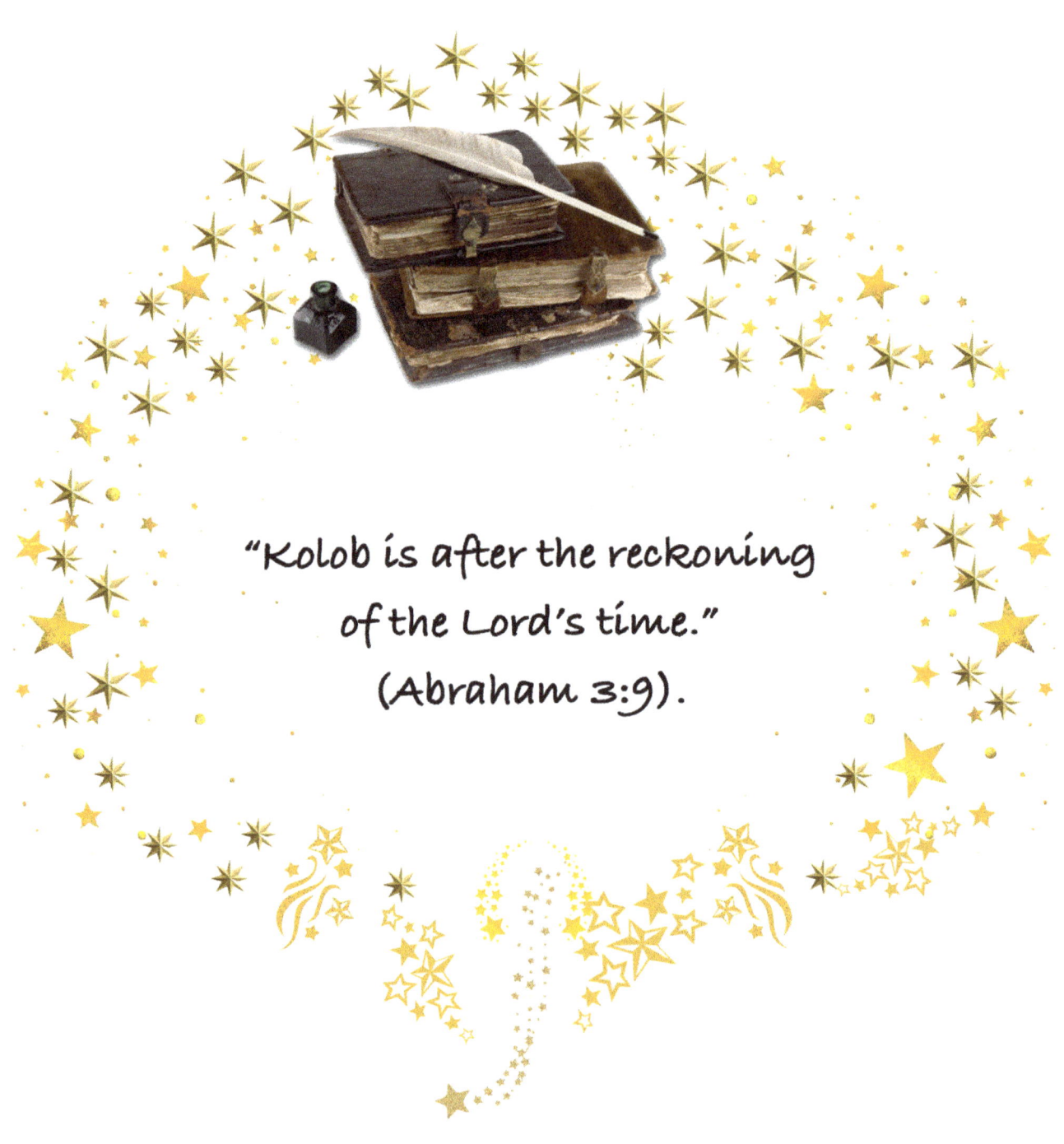

"Kolob is after the reckoning of the Lord's time." (Abraham 3:9).

When we
look up into space, we
are looking back in time.
The light arriving at Earth
from the farthest objects in the
universe has been zipping across
the cosmos for billions of years.
We see them not as they really
are, but only as they were
long ago.

For the moment, we
are trapped within the matrix
of time, and seconds, minutes, and
hours are the glue that binds us to the
fabric of mortality. Thus, we can
only indirectly appreciate
the eternities.

If we could
unravel the mysteries
surrounding the complex
matrix of life that is teeming
in air, on land, and within the
ocean deeps, there might lie before
us, like an open book, the tangible
evidence of a continuity of existence
without temporal or spatial boundaries;
one that instead thrives on energy that
is felt throughout the galaxy. Though
the origin of the expression "May the
Force be with you." is traceable to
imaginary extra-terrestrials,
it is still one with which
we are all familiar.

"Kolob is set nigh unto the throne of God, to govern all those planets which belong to the same order as that upon which thou standest." (Abraham 3:9).

Civilizations
in the cosmos that have
achieved a reconciliation with
Jesus Christ will relinquish to
Him control over their home
worlds, their star systems,
and their galaxies, as
well as kingdoms
of glory.

"I can never look at the
Milky Way without wondering
from which of those banked clouds of
stars the emissaries are coming. We have
set off the fire alarm, and have nothing
to do but wait. I do not think we
will have to wait for long."
(Arthur C. Clarke).

If we refuse to acknowledge the
certain reality that we are not alone
in the universe, that its Master lives out
there somewhere beyond the Trail to Mount
Olympus, where will we find sanctuary when
the winds blow, and the rains beat down? To
what safe harbor will we flee when the ocean
of life is in turmoil? If we are tossed about
as flotsam and jetsam, but never come
to a knowledge of what is true, to what
source will we look for the stability
we so desperately seek? Where will
we find the answers to life's
greatest questions, that
continually trouble
our spirits?

"There shall be the reckoning of the time of one planet above another, until thou come nigh unto Kolob." (Abraham 3:9).

"The universe doesn't
make things in "ones". Is the
Earth special, and everything else is
different? No. There are 7 other planets.
The Sun? No. It's one of those dots in the
night sky. The Milky Way? No. It's one of
600 billion galaxies. And the universe?
Maybe it's one of countless others."
(Neil deGrasse Tyson).

"When I trace the
paths of heavenly bodies, I
no longer touch the earth with
my feet. I stand in the presence
of Zeus himself, and take
my fill of ambrosia"
(Ptolemy).

As eternity
bursts upon us, we will
surely be dazzled by an expanded
appreciation of our relationship with
the Savior, both temporally and spiritually.
It may only then dawn upon us that when He
described Himself as the Light of the World, He may
have been speaking literally as well as figuratively. In
the physical world, time shifts compensate for our velocities
relative to beams of light. In the eternal world, time shifts so
completely in relation to our Redeemer, that it is no more, and
the cosmic speed limit becomes a negligible influence. Thanks
to Albert Einstein, we realize it's all relative! Thanks to our
Heavenly Father's utilization of eternal law, there is a
reconciliation between time and being that erases
the cosmic speed limit while, at the same time,
easing our transition into the eternities.

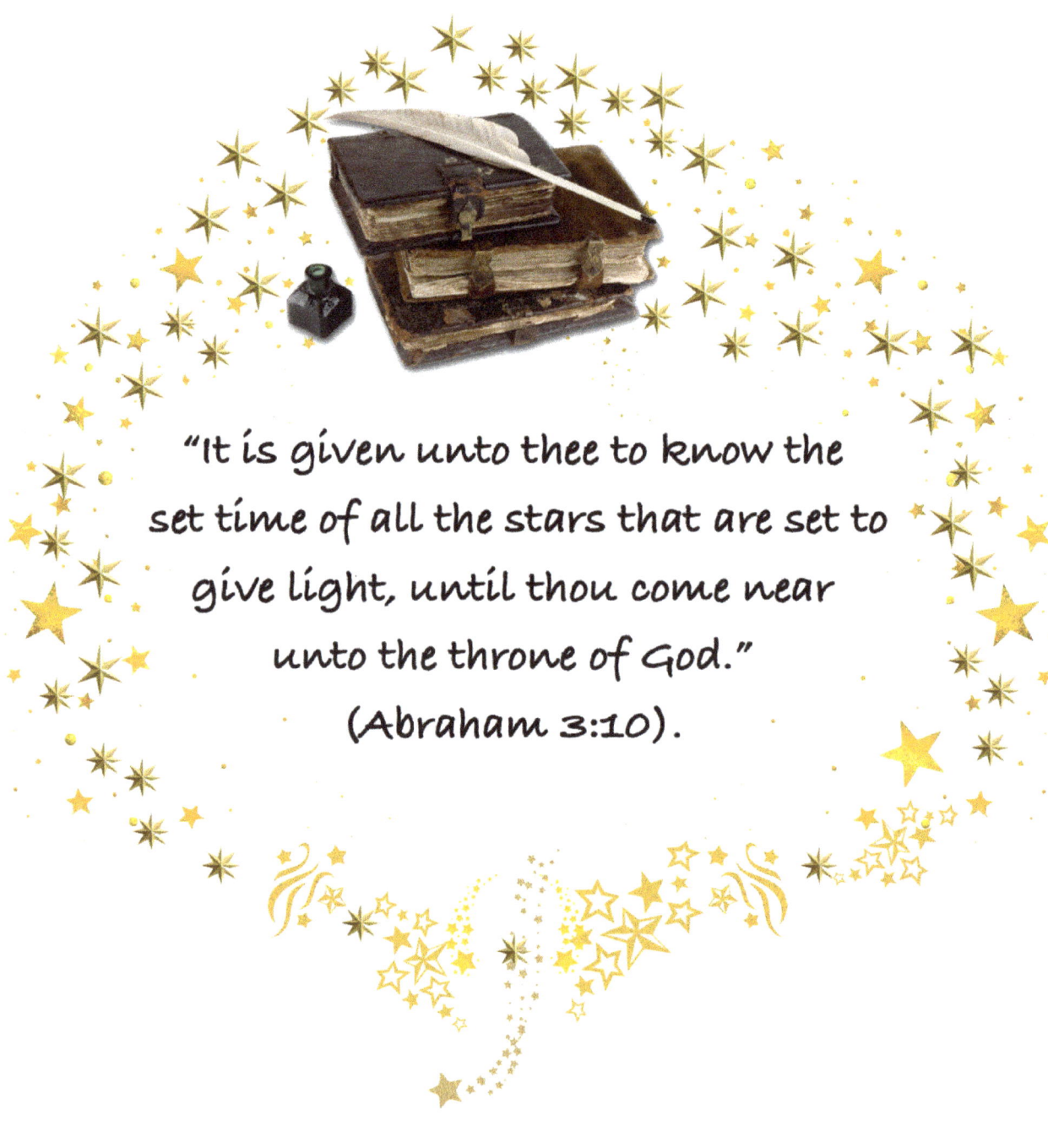

"It is given unto thee to know the set time of all the stars that are set to give light, until thou come near unto the throne of God." (Abraham 3:10).

In an episode of Star Trek Voyager, a character declares: "The past, the present, and the future exist as one. They breathe together." Our Father "hath given a law unto all things. By him they move in their times and their seasons. And their courses are fixed, even the courses of the heavens and the earth. All these are one … with God."
(D&C 88:42-44).

At the Second Coming of the Lord, the Saints will experience a dramatic manifestation of spatial transference when they are "caught up together … in the clouds, to meet the Lord in the air."
(1 Thessalonians 4:17).

Left to our own devices, we will never understand the physical universe so completely that we will ever become its master. We cannot presume to supplant God's intellect with our own. We can never, in any significant way, understand the eternities while we remain within a stew of seconds, the mire of minutes, and the agony of hours. Well did the Psalmist counsel: "Be still, and know that I am God."
(Psalms 46:10).

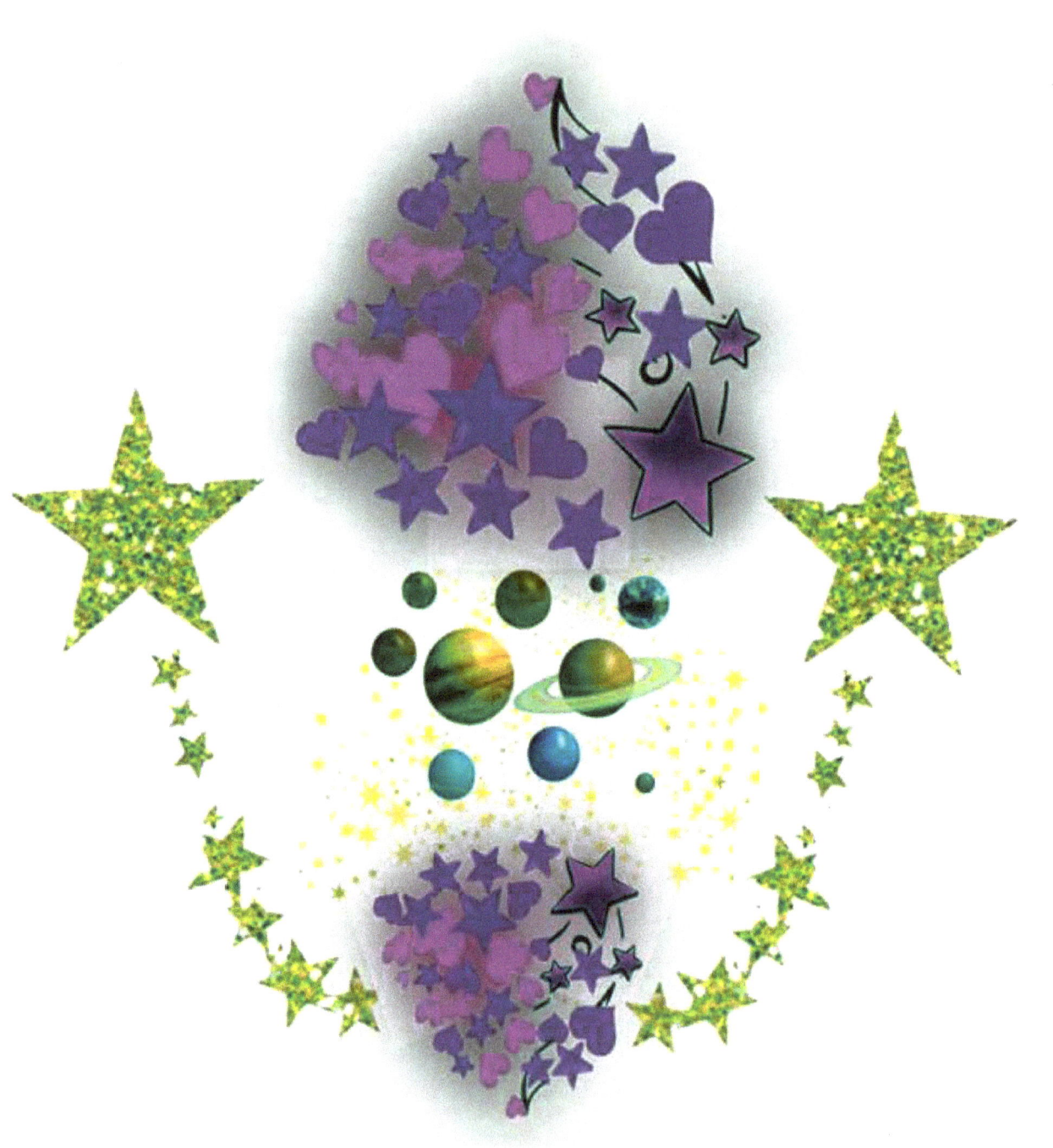

"He saw the heavens open, and he thought he saw God sitting upon his throne surrounded with numberless concourses of angels." (1 Nephi 1:8).

Captain Jean
Luc Picard declared:
"Considering the marvelous
complexity of the universe, its
clockwork perfection, and its
balance between matter, energy,
gravitation, time, and dimension,
I believe that our existence must go
beyond Euclidean or other practical
measuring systems, and that
it is part of a reality beyond
what we now understand."

If warp drive
technology could create
an artificial "bubble" of normal
space-time surrounding a star ship,
the vehicle would be able to maintain
interaction with objects in normal space,
while at warp speed. A theoretical solution for
faster-than-light travel that models the warp
drive concept has scientists conducting
preliminary research to learn more
about the practical applications
of this technology.

Our native consciousness,
or its equivalent that exists somewhere
out there among the stars, might one day be
downloaded into a virtual or augmented reality
environment. If this process could physically and
psychologically alter the perception of the passage
of time, it might render as feasible interstellar
voyages of extended duration, even if they
took millennia to complete.

"He is the same yesterday, today, and forever, and the way is prepared for all men from the foundation of the world."

(1 Nephi 10:18).

Time flies like an arrow,
and fruit flies like
ripe bananas.

At the dawn of the 20th
century, it had taken 150
years to double all human
knowledge. Today, it takes
only around 12 months,
and soon it will be every
12 hours, according to
reliable estimates.

Since the 1970s,
the Information Age, also
known as the Digital Age, Computer
Age, or New Media Age, has 'blessed' our
lives with a shift from industrialization
to information computerization and a
knowledge-based society embedded
within a global economy.

Without intentionally
doing so, Steven Hawking hinted
at our relationship with the ticking clock
that is calibrated to a celestial scale: "The theory
of gravity," he said, "has created new possibilities,
in which there is no boundary to space-time … The
boundary condition of the universe is that it has no
boundary." He may as well have been describing
eternity, which is unique, although it does share
surprising similarities to the theoretical view of
time proffered by quantum mechanics. It is
an open system that cannot be defined
by temporal or spatial borders.

"It must needs be an infinite atonement." (2 Nephi 9:7).

At the end of the world,
when the veil that has been drawn
across our minds evaporates, time will
be no more, and as we ease into eternity,
we will become increasingly comfortable
with our reconciliation to the native
and more natural environment
of our former home.

Time and space, and
even reality, are the final
frontiers. This is the voyage
of humanity. Its continuing
mission: To explore strange new
worlds, to seek out new life
and new civilizations, to
boldly go where no one
has gone before.

From the
perspective of God,
the arrow of time moves in
all directions. It is only our stable
temporal frame of reference that allows
us to live within a timeline that overlays the
tapestry of our familiar three-dimensional space.
It reassures us that the sun will come up tomorrow,
and that there will be 24 hours in each day to address
life's challenges. Without the veil that insulates us from
God's unrestrained, unencumbered, unreserved, and
uninhibited temporal reality, which is His ever
present "now", life would surely be very
confusing, and mortality would
lose its razor-edge.

"If there be no Christ there be no God; and if there be no God we are not, for there could have been no creation."
(2 Nephi 11:7).

"Of all the communities that are available to us, there is not one that I would want to devote myself to, except for the society of true searchers, which has very few living members at any one time."
(Albert Einstein).

Beings from the unseen world may exist in a parallel, or perhaps a higher, spatial dimension, which may be for them like our being in a room with a one way mirror. They may witness our every day world on a whim, but to those of us trapped in the here-and-now, trying to see what lies in the other 'direction' beyond the mirror's reflective surface is fruitless.

Traveling at the speed of light, it would take at least 94 billion years to traverse the known universe. Plodding along at light speed from point A to point B seems unlikely because those of us who have gotten the Lord's attention know that His intercession can be instantaneous, no matter to what corner of the universe our pleas may have traveled to reach His ear.

"There is nothing which is secret save it shall be revealed ... and there is nothing which is sealed upon the earth, save it shall be loosed."
(2 Nephi 30:17).

As we cry out to Him,
God hears us with the power to
immediately respond to our needs,
wherever and whenever He or we may be.
Existing in another dimension gives God the
ability to hear our petitions simultaneously,
without the inherent limitations of three
dimensional space, time warps
notwithstanding.

Sensing his astonishment, the Lord
counseled Moses: "The heavens they are many,
and they cannot be numbered unto man; but they
are numbed unto me, for they are mine." (Moses
1:36). Clearly, we are dealing with two orders of
mind, that of mortals, and that of God. "My
thoughts are not your thoughts, neither are
your ways my ways, saith the Lord.
For as the heavens are higher than
the earth, so are ... my thoughts
than your thoughts."
(Isaiah 55:8-9).

Meet Joe Black
was a film that was loosely based
on the 1934 motion picture "Death Takes
a Holiday." At its conclusion, the protagonist,
who is about to die, asks Death: "Should I be afraid?"
When Death answers him and says: "Not a man like
you," we know that, in the face of the inevitable,
everything is going to be okay. May we so live
that when it is our time to reach out and
touch the stars, and to feel the warm
embrace of heaven, we will be
similarly blessed.

"By the power of his word man came upon the face of the earth, which earth was created by the power of his word." (Jacob 4:9).

God
invites us to follow
Him along a trajectory
that will take us across the
galaxy. It is prefaced by the
verb "to come." The question
is: If we come follow Him,
where and when and how
far will that journey
take us?

Spiritual
enlightenment can
create a celestial bridge
that transports us past the
improbabilities of life to the
stability of understanding,
not only of this world, but
also of the world that lies
beyond the horizon.

After we have kept our second
estate, and have had glory added upon
our heads, what will we be like? What does it
mean to be clothed with immortality and eternal
life? Will we then more closely resemble our Father
in Heaven in both His image and His likeness? If so,
could we, even now, be gods and goddesses in embryo?
If that is true, does it not then mean our genetic code is
divine? Is it our destiny to mature to the stature of our
Heavenly Parents? When we are born again, is it a
process of maturation, or of generation? Can we
become new creatures in Christ? Can the
universe really be a machine for
the making of gods?

"The Son of God cometh in his glory, in his might, majesty, power and dominion." (Alma 5:50).

The Atonement of
Jesus Christ was not in vain. We
are anxiously engaged, hungering and
thirsting after righteousness, boldly declaring
the Gospel, and with fear and trembling working
out our salvation before Him. We are carried away on
the wings of the Spirit to visions of glory. We continue
to smite the destroyer with the power of the word, we
live life with divine fire, and we are confident
that we will one day be caught up to engage
a mission to explore strange new worlds,
to seek new life and new civilizations,
and to boldly go where no-one
has gone before.

If life exists elsewhere
in the galaxy, we have no way of
determining whether it is charitable
in nature and is motivated by the celestial
principles that have guided those who inhabit
our Pale Blue Dot to be honest, true, chaste, and
benevolent, virtuous, lovely, and of good report.
But of one thing we are certain: those of us
whose lives are fueled by faith march to the
beat of a different drummer. Our real
journey to the stars is propelled
by the foundation, fabric,
and focus of faith.

If our precious vessels
of oil are never replenished,
they will be empty at the day
of reckoning when First
Contact is made with
the Spirit.

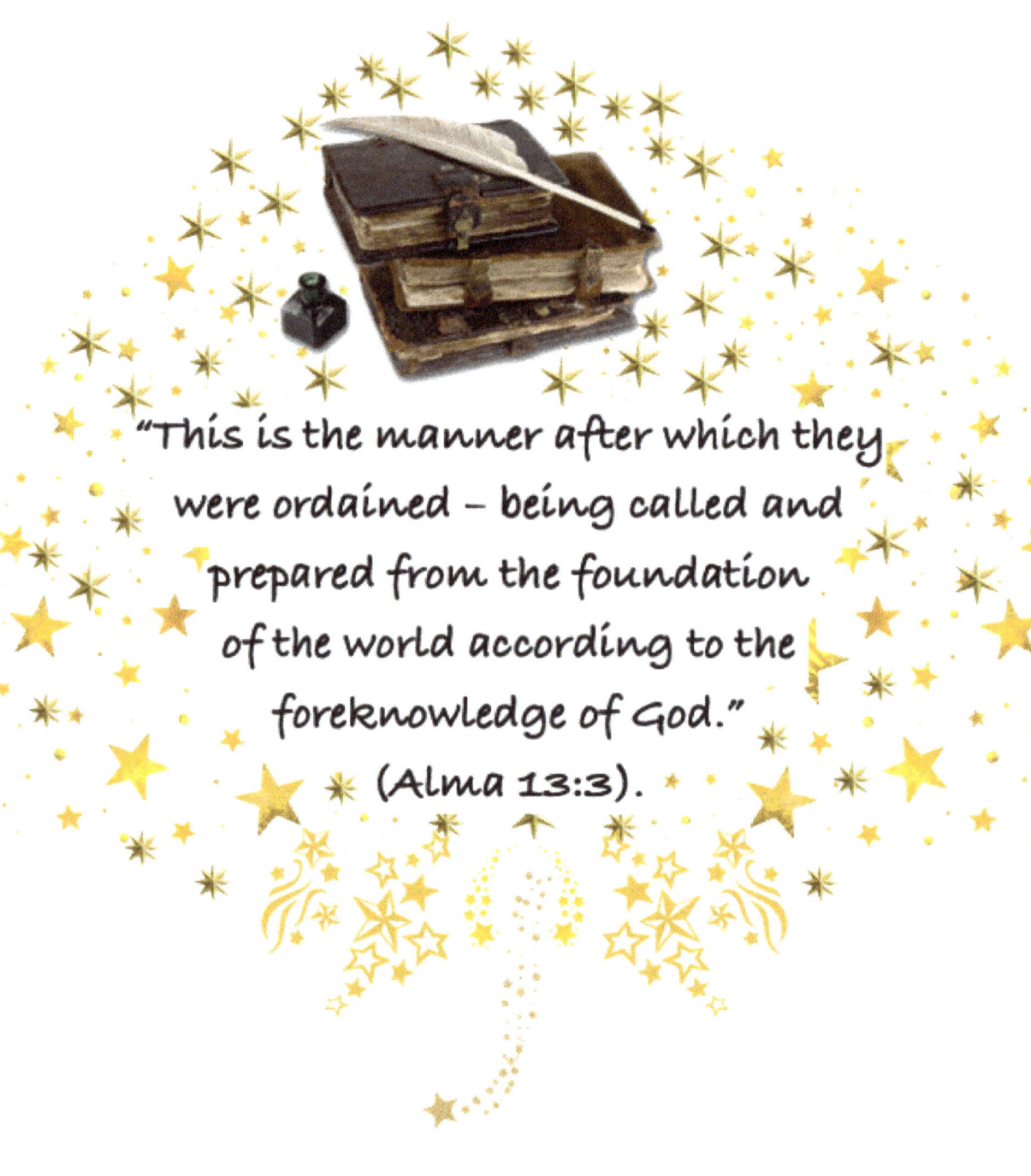

"This is the manner after which they were ordained – being called and prepared from the foundation of the world according to the foreknowledge of God." (Alma 13:3).

"We choose to go to the Moon," declared President John F. Kennedy in May 1961, "not because it is easy, but because it is hard, because that goal will serve to organize and measure the best of our energies and skills, because that challenge is one that we are willing to accept, one we are unwilling to postpone, and one that we intend to win." Fifty years later, we've been to the Moon. It is time to stir up that fire in our bones and set our sights on heaven.

If we ever hope to understand the mystery of mysteries and to be at peace with our place in the cosmos, we must read, fear, hope, and pray. We must lift the latch and force the way, as Sir Walter Scott suggested. We must expend soul sweat, and our inspiration must be preceded by perspiration, because our enlightenment, in order to be meaningful, must be deserved. It must be earned line upon line, and precept upon precept, only after payment with the equity of exercise. It cannot come freely to those who wander the cosmos, who are tossed to and fro by every wind of doctrine, because they lack the discipline of faith by which The Plan of Salvation is able to bless all of the teachable children of our Heavenly Father.

Trans-warp drive, spore drive, subspace, coaxial space, and even travel at the speed of thought will not bring us as close to God as will simply dropping to our knees in prayer. That simple exercise, and not the omega particle, or the quantum slipstream drive, will bless us with the strength to draw upon the ultimate Power Source in the universe.

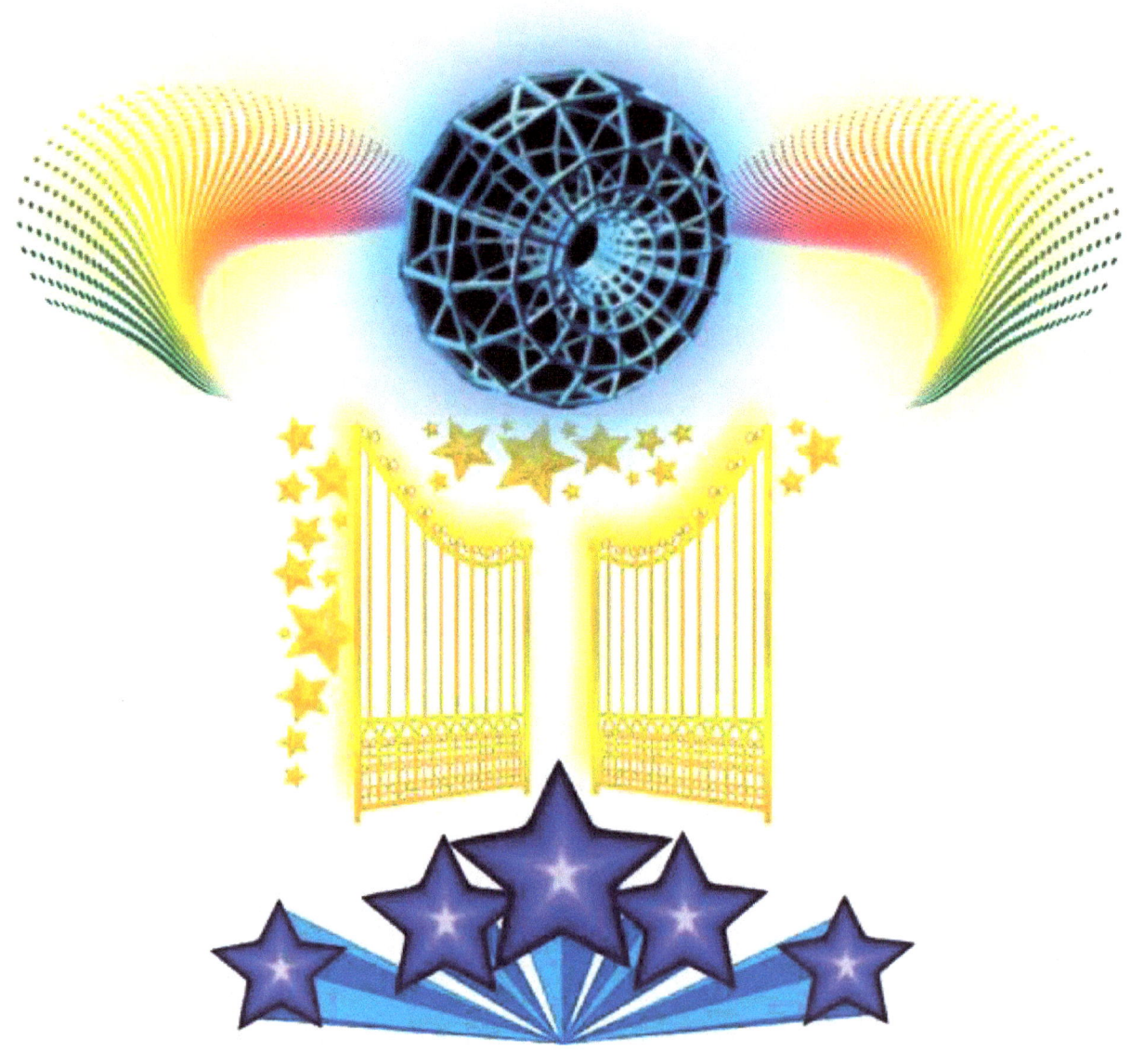

"It is by faith that angels appear and minister unto men."

(Moroni 7:37).

The universe won't collapse because of
the dark energy that is pushing it apart.
Eventually, however, it will become a dilute
mist of iron atoms at a temperature that
approaches absolute zero. Fortunately,
this will not happen until it is
several trillion times older
than it is now.

The
interstellar medium is
of interest to astronomers, in
part, because it is the spawning
ground of stars as well as the place
where they deposit newly created
chemical elements, that future
generations of stars and
planets inherit as
their building
blocks.

Voyager 1 has become the
first spacecraft from Earth to cross
the heliopause to reach interstellar space, but
it has not really left the solar system. Roughly a
trillion icy bodies revolve around the Sun far beyond
the orbits of Neptune and Pluto, and every now and then
when one of them plunges toward the Sun, we see a new comet
in the sky. The farthest of these distant frigid objects are one or
two light-years away. If you were standing in the center of the
continental United States, two miles northwest of Lebanon,
Kansas, and walked three miles west, you would have
gotten closer to the Pacific Ocean, relatively
speaking, than has Voyager 1 gotten to
the edge of the solar system.

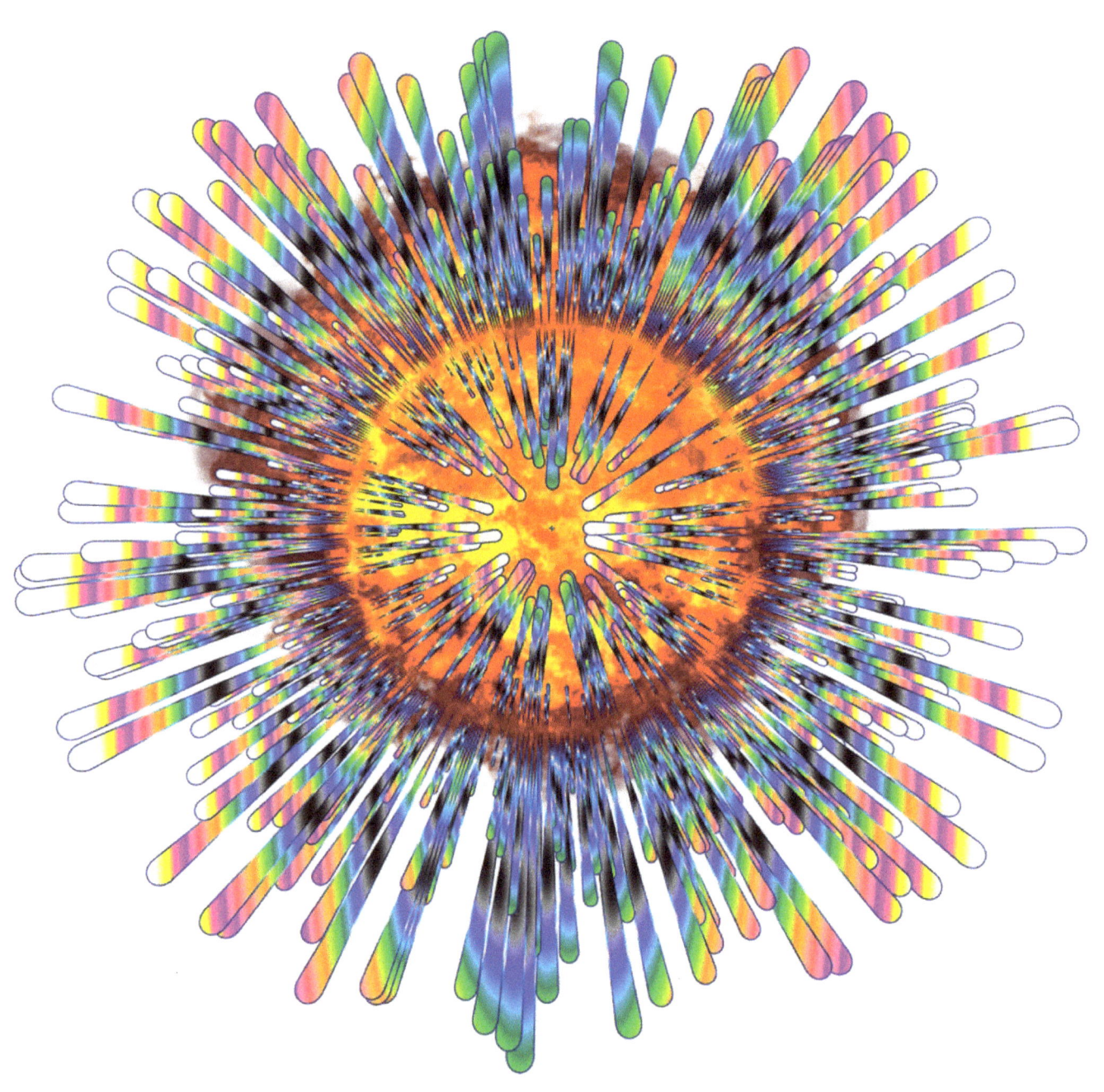

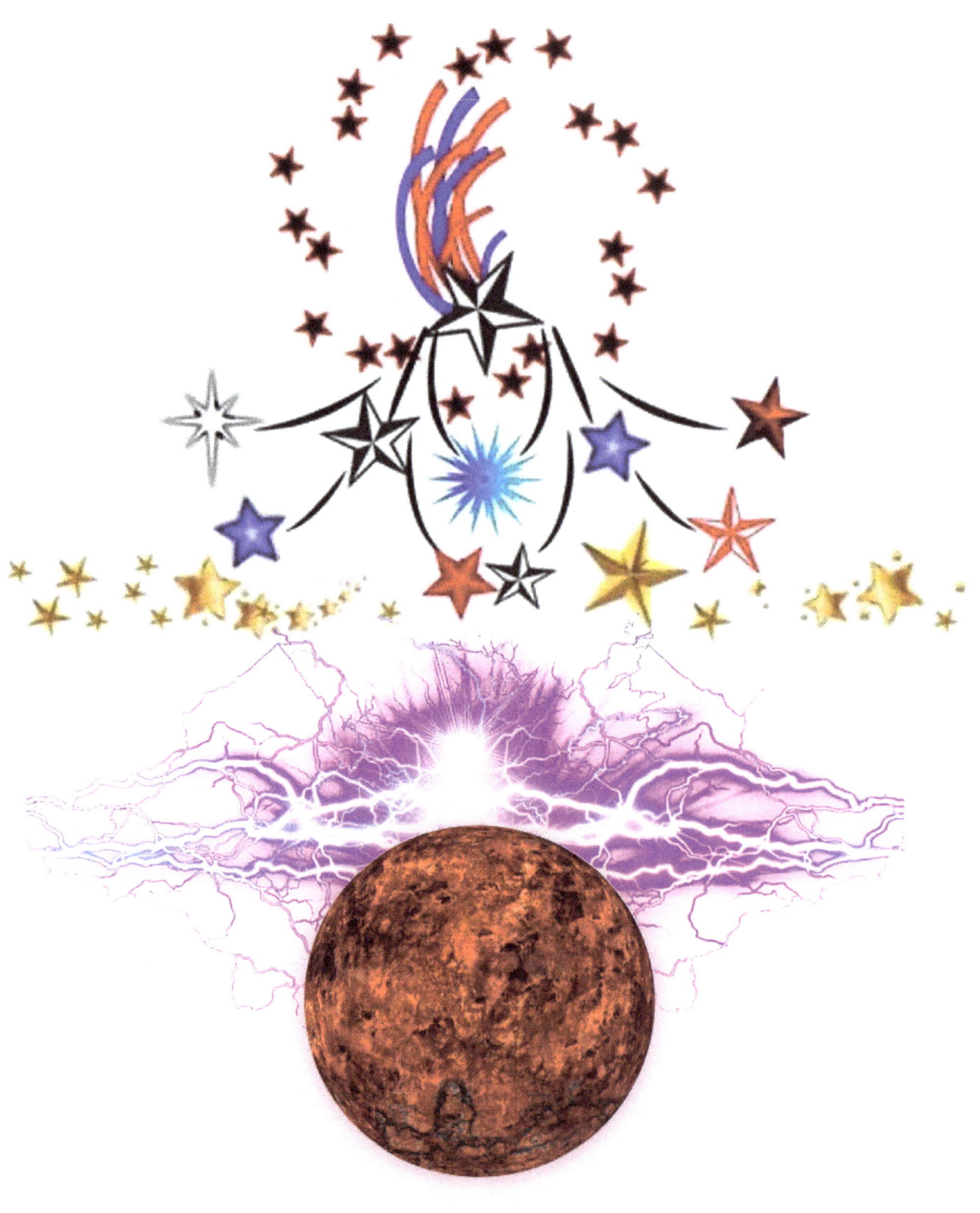

Epilogue

"I am the Lord thy God;
I dwell in heaven; the earth is my
footstool; I stretch my hand over the sea,
and it obeys my voice; I cause the wind
and the fire to be my chariot."
(Abraham 2:7).

'I say to the mountains -
Depart hence - and behold, they
are taken away by a whirlwind,
in an instant, suddenly."
(Abraham 2:7).

It is both humbling
and character building
to probe the far reaches of
the universe, not to mention
the depths of eternity, and to
realize that those who are aboard
Spaceship Earth are on a very
small vessel navigating a
vast cosmic ocean.

We learn in
D&C 76:112 that those
in a lower kingdom cannot
move, of their own accord, into a
higher kingdom any more than we
could, by our own efforts, move from
three dimensions into four. For
them or for us to do so would
require the intervention
of a higher power.

We are generally locked on
telestial targets and cannot see
the forest for the trees. We look at the
Milky Way and count its stars, rather
than our blessings. We content ourselves
to be governed by a rev-limiter on the power
plant that fuels not only our cars, but also
galaxies, and the heavens. We are drawn
to the light like moths are to fire, but
we flutter around without purpose
and direction. Too often, higher
level thinking seems to be
beyond the reach of our
comprehension.

Appendix One

Scriptures that are cited in Volumes One, Two, Three, and Four

Dancing With the Stars – Volume One

D&C 76:7	D&C 132:30	Isaiah 45:3
D&C 76:9	D&C 138:56	Isaiah 54:2
D&C 76:10	D&C 138:57	Isaiah 55:8
D&C 76:25	Numbers 16:32	Isaiah 55:9
D&C 76:39	Deuteronomy 32:8	Jeremiah 1:5
D&C 76:91	Psalms 8:6	Matthew 3:16
D&C 76:96	Psalms 91:1	Luke 1:33
D&C 76:97	Psalms 102:5	Titus 1:2
D&C 76:98	Psalms 104:1-2	1 Peter 1:19-20
D&C 76:109	Psalms 104:3	Abraham 4:8
D&C 92:23	Psalms 104:4-4	Enos 1:27
D&C 92:29	Psalms 145:13	Mosiah 4:2
D&C 109:77	Psalms 147:5	3 Nephi 9:15
D&C 121:29	Ecclesiastes 12:7	3 Nephi 28:36
D&C 121:30	Isaiah 9:7	Ether 3:16
D&C 121:31	Isaiah 13:13	Ether 3:25
D&C 121:32	Isaiah 34:4	Mormon 7:29-30
D&C 130:8	Isaiah 40:22	Moroni 7:28
D&C 131:1	Isaiah 42:5	

Dancing With the Stars – Volume Two

D&C 21:6	Isaiah 34:4	Moses 1:28
D&C 29:33	Isaiah 64:8	Moses 1:33
D&C 35:1	Ezekiel 1:5-6	Moses 1:37
D&C 35:2	Daniel 2:28	Moses 3:5
D&C 76:24	Daniel 4:3	Moses 6:36
D&C 78:14	Daniel 7:13	Moses 7:30
D&C 88:7	Daniel 7:13-14	Moses 7:36
D&C 88:95	Daniel 10:5-6	Abraham 3:9
D&C 88:97	Amos 3:7	Abraham 3:10
D&C 93:10	Matthew 13:35	1 Nephi 1:8
Genesis 1:1-2	John 1:3	1 Nephi 10:18
Deuteronomy 30:14	John 1:51	2 Nephi 9:7
Job 38:6-7	Romans 8:16	2 Nephi 11:7
Psalms 8:3-4	Acts 17:26	2 Nephi 30:17
Psalms 104:4-5	Ephesians 3:21	Jacob 4:9
Psalms 145:13	Revelation 21:1	Alma 5:50
Psalms 147:5	Moses 1:3	Alma 13:3
Proverbs 15:3	Moses 1:8	Moroni 7:37
Isaiah 13:13		

Dancing With the Stars – Volume Three

- D&C 93:10
- D&C 93:10
- D&C 133:69
- Deuteronomy 10:14
- Deuteronomy 29:29
- Deuteronomy 30:14
- 2 Kinga 1:10
- 2 Kings 2:11
- Job 38:4-5
- Job 38:33
- Psalms 8:3-4
- Psalms 33:6
- Psalms 91:1
- Proverbs 15:3
- Isaiah 42:5
- Isaiah 45:3
- Isaiah 54:2
- Jeremiah 14:22
- Jeremiah 16:23
- Jeremiah 31:35
- Jeremiah 51:15
- Ezekiel 1:4
- Amos 3:7
- Amos 4:13
- Micah 1:3
- Micah 1:4
- Matthew 13:35
- Matthew 24:31
- Luke 8:17
- John 1:3
- John 1:51
- Acts 1:11
- Acts 2:3
- Acts 4:24
- Acts 9:3
- Acts 10:11
- Ephesians 1:21
- Ephesians 3:21
- Hebrews 1:2
- Hebrews 1:10
- Hebrews 7:26
- Hebrews 10:34
- Hebrews 11:3
- 2 Peter 3:10
- Revelation 4:11
- Revelation 6:14
- Revelation 21:1
- Moses 1:38
- 1 Nephi 5:11
- Mosiah 7:28
- Mosiah 16:9
- Helaman 5:48
- 3 Nephi 26:3
- Mormon 5:23
- Mormon 9:2
- Moroni 10:34

Dancing With the Stars - Volume Four

D&C 3:2	D&C 133:69	2 Timothy 1:9
D&C 14:9	Deuteronomy 29:26	Hebrews 7:26
D&C 20:17	Psalms 8:6	Hebrews 10:34
D&C 20:18	Psalms 33:6	Hebrews 11:3
D&C 45:1	Psalms 102:5	Revelation 6:14
D&C 49:17	Psalms 104:1-2	Moses 2:1
D&C 62:3	Psalms 104:3	Abraham 3:14
D&C 88:7	Isaiah 40:22	Abraham 2:22
D&C 88:37	Jeremiah 23:24	Abraham 3:24
D&C 88:38	Jeremiah 51:15	Abraham 3:26
D&C 88:42	Acts 14:23	1 Nephi 10:19
D&C 88:43	Acts 17:26	2 Nephi 2:14
D&C 88:44	Romans 8:38-39	Alma 13:7
D&C 88:47	1 Corinthians 2:9	Alma 13:9
D&C 88:95	1 Corinthians 2:10	Alma 18:30
D&C 88:97	2 Corinthians 2:12	Alma 34:10
D&C 130:8	Ephesians 1:4	Alma 37:11
D&C 131:1	Colossians 1:16	

About The Author

Phil Hudson and his wife Jan have 7 children and 25 grandchildren. They enjoy spending time with their family at their cabin nestled in the Selkirk Mountains, on the shore of Priest Lake, the crown jewel of North Idaho. Phil had a successful dental practice in Spokane, Washington for 43 years, before retiring in 2015. He has an eclectic mix of hobbies and enjoys the out of doors. He always finds time, however, to record his thoughts on his laptop, and understands Isaac Asimov's response when he was asked: "If you knew that you had only 10 minutes left to live, what would you do?" He answered: "I'd type faster."

Phil received the inspiration to write this book while he and Jan were serving as missionaries for The Church of Jesus Christ of Latter-day Saints, in the Kingdom of Tonga. While there, they celebrated their 50th wedding anniversary.

By The Author

Essays

- Volume 1 - Spray from The Ocean of Thought
- Volume 2 - Ripples on a Pond
- Volume 3 - Serendipitous Meanderings
- Volume 4 - Presents of Mind
- Volume 5 - Mental Floss
- Volume 6 - Fitness Training for the Mind and Spirit

First Principles and Ordinances Series

- Faith - Our Hearts are Changed
- Repentance - A Broken Heart and a Contrite Spirit
- Baptism - One Hundred and One Reasons Why We Are Baptized
- Holy Ghost - That We Might Have His Spirit to Be With Us
- Sacrament - This Do in Remembrance of Me

Minute Musings - Spontaneous Combustions of Thought

- Volume One
- Volume Two
- Volume Three

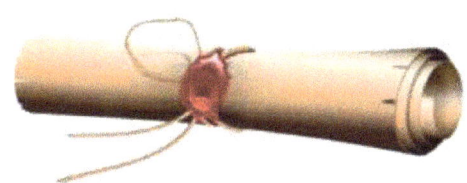  

Book of Mormon Commentary

- Volume One - Born in The Wilderness
- Volume Two - Voices from The Dust
- Volume Three - Journey to Cumorah

Calendars

- In His Own Words - Discovering William Tyndale
- As I Think About the Savior
- Daily Inspiration from Scriptural Symbols

A Thought for Each Day of the Year

- Faith
- Repentance
- Baptism
- The Holy Ghost
- The Sacrament
- Life's Greatest Questions
- Revelation
- The Atonement
- The House of the Lord
- The Plan of Salvation
- The Sabbath

Doctrine & Covenants Commentary

- Volume One - Sections 1 - 34
- Volume Two - Sections 35 - 57

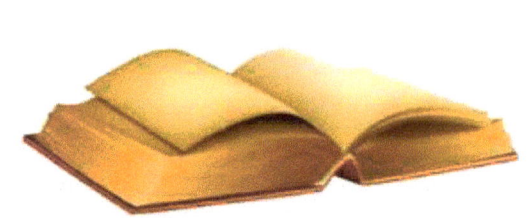

Doctrinal Themes

- Are Christians Mormon? – Volume One
- Are Christians Mormon? – Volume Two
- Are We Alone in The Universe? – Volume One
- Are We Alone in The Universe? – Volume Two
- Christmas is The Season When ...
- Dancing With the Stars – Volume One
- Dancing With the Stars – Volume Two
- Dancing With the Stars – Volume Three
- Dancing With the Stars – Volume Four
- Dentistry in The Scriptures
- Gratitude
- Hebrew Poetry
- Hiding in Plain Sight
- One Hundred Questions Answered by The Book of Mormon
- The Highways and Byways of Life – Volume One
- The Highways and Byways of Life – Volume Two
- The Highways and Byways of Life – Volume Three
- The House of The Lord
- Without the Book of Mormon
- Writing on Metal Plates

Children's Books

- Book of Mormon Hiking Song – Volume One
- Book of Mormon Hiking Song – Volume Two
- Book of Mormon Hiking Song – Volume Three
- Happy Birthday
- Muddy, Muddy

The Hiawatha Trail - An Allegory
The Little Princess
The Parable of The Pencil
The Strange Tale of Huckleberry Henry
The Thirteen Articles of Faith

Professional Publications

Diode Laser Soft Tissue Surgery – Volume One
Diode Laser Soft Tissue Surgery – Volume Two
Diode Laser Soft Tissue Surgery – Volume Three

These, and other titles, are available from online retailers.

Quid Magis Possum Dicire?